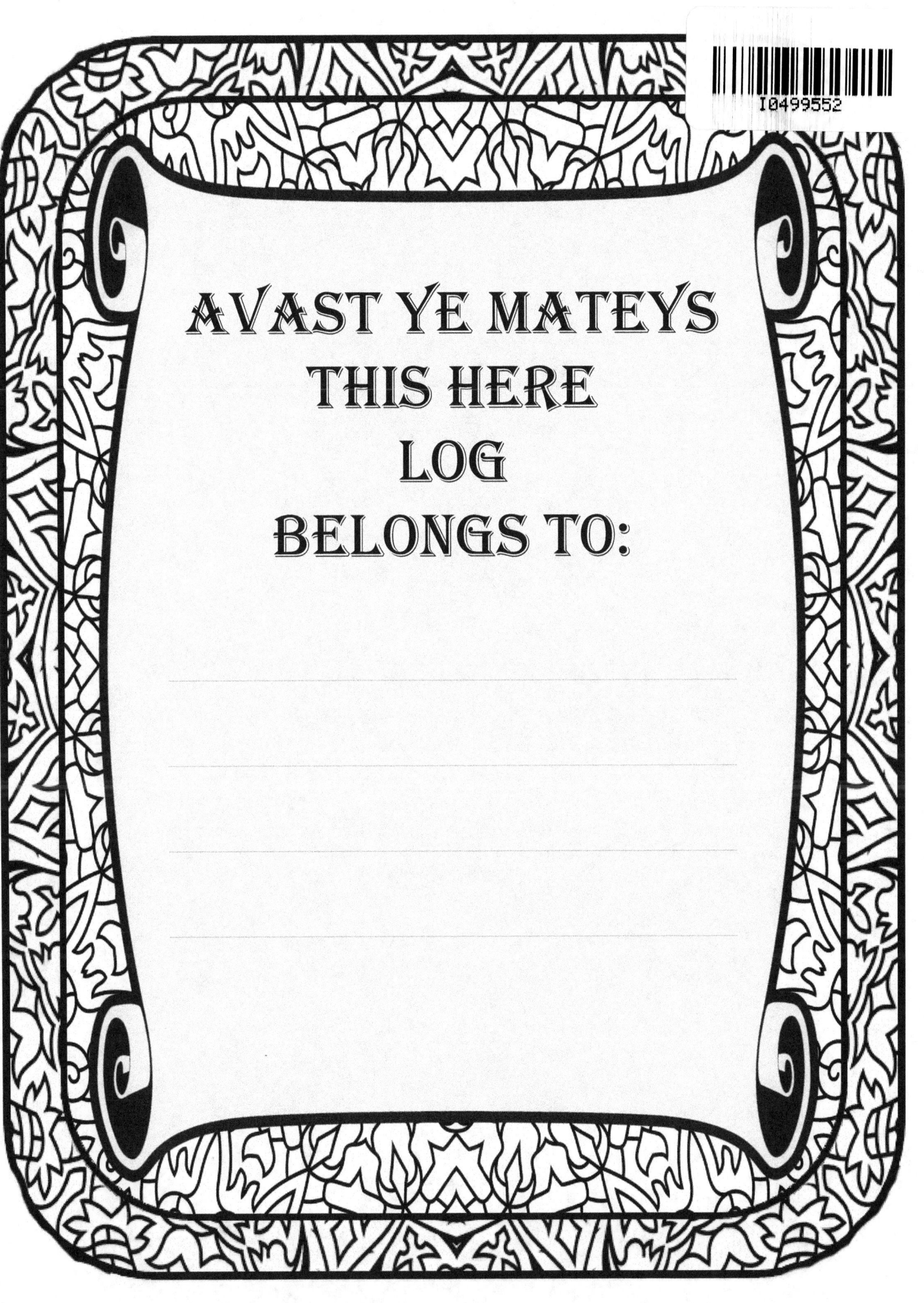

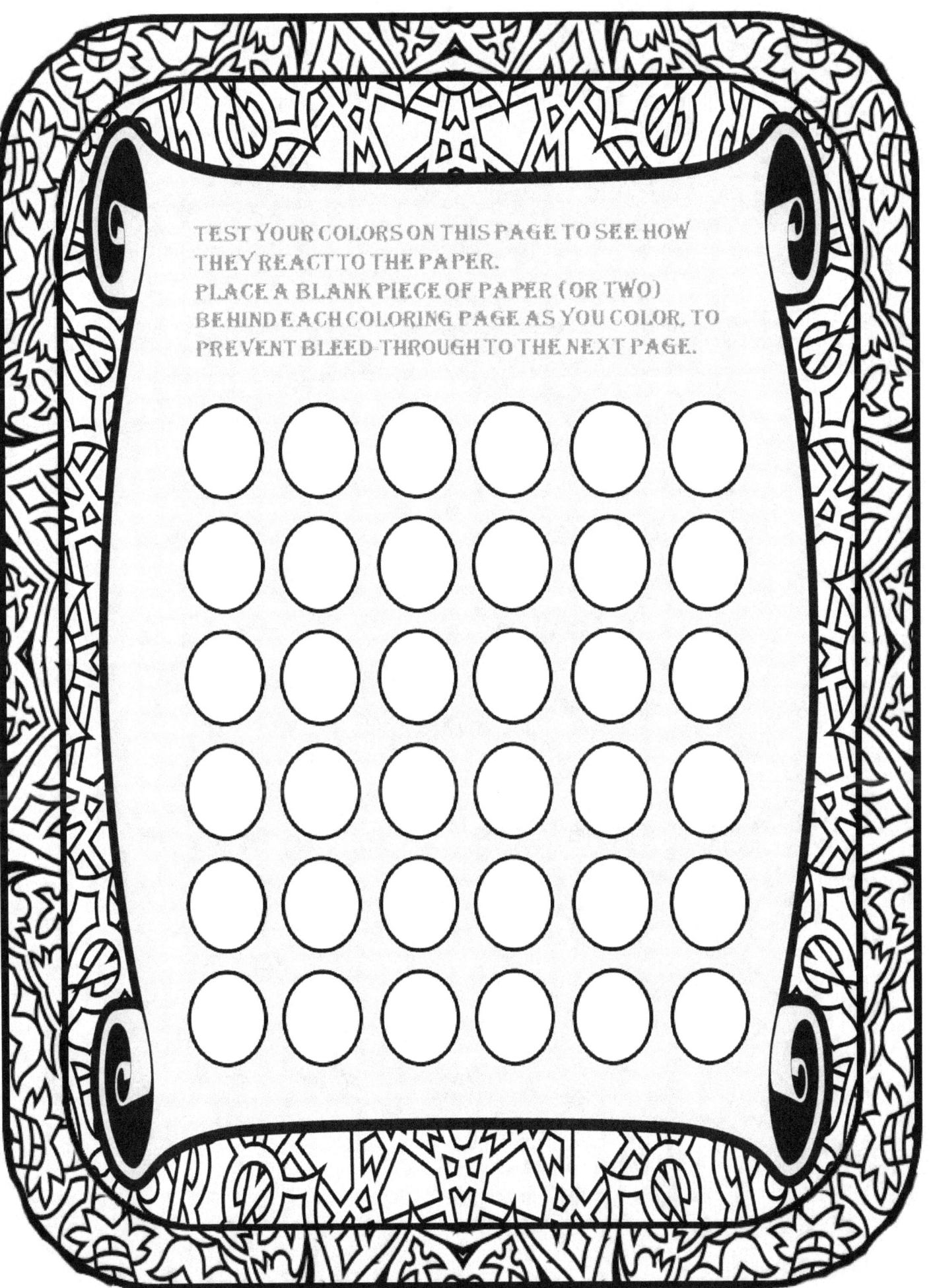

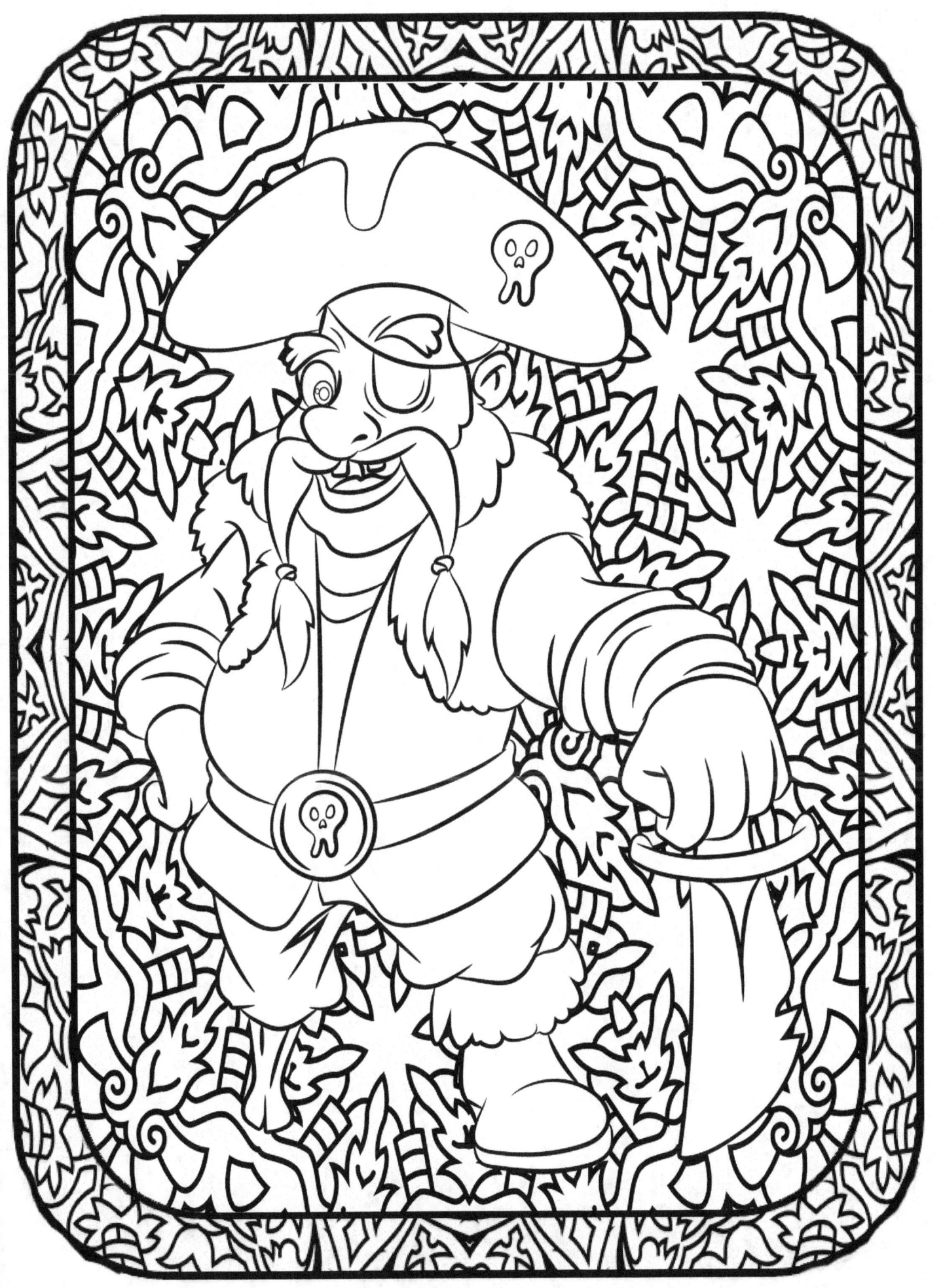

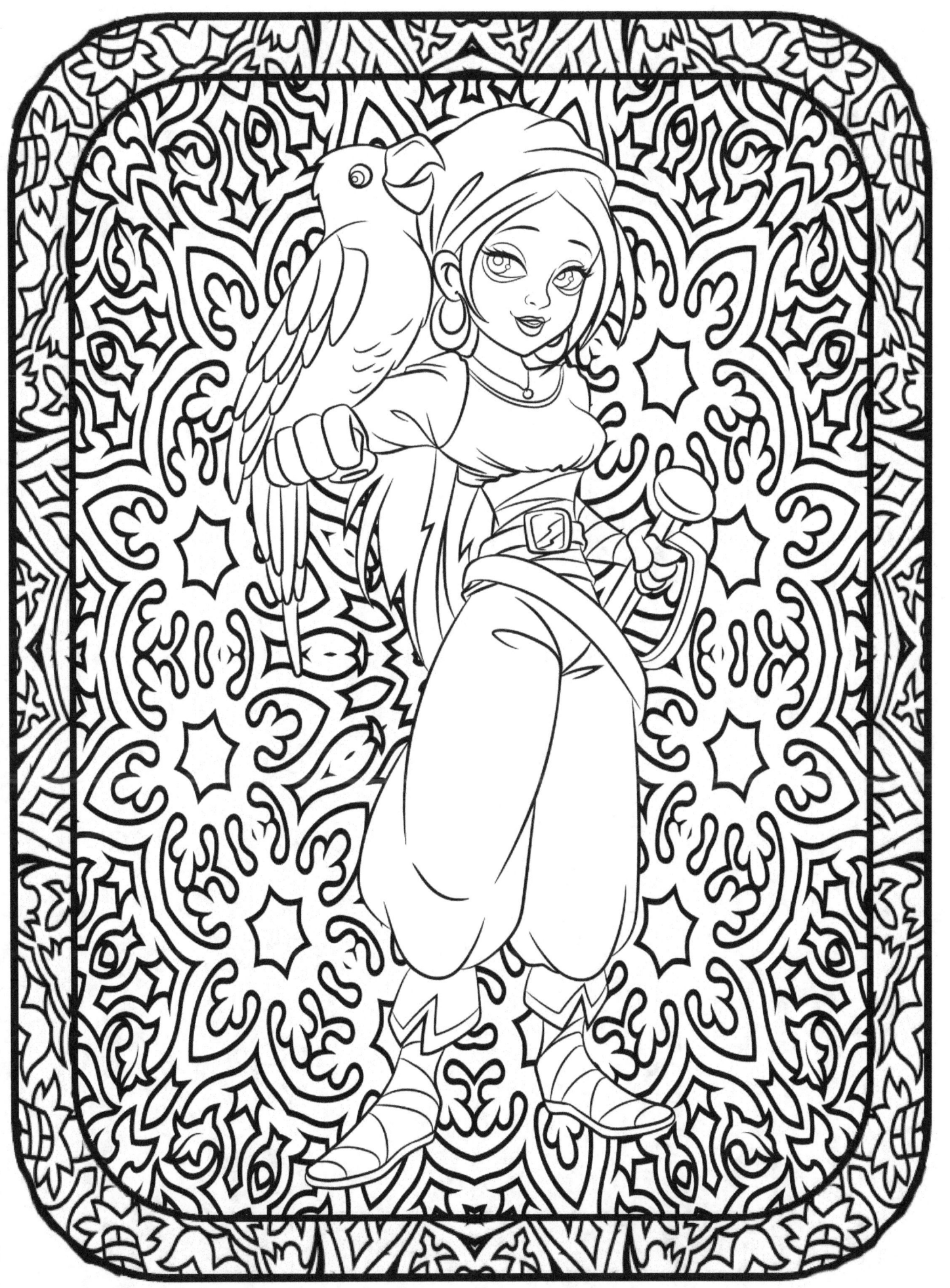

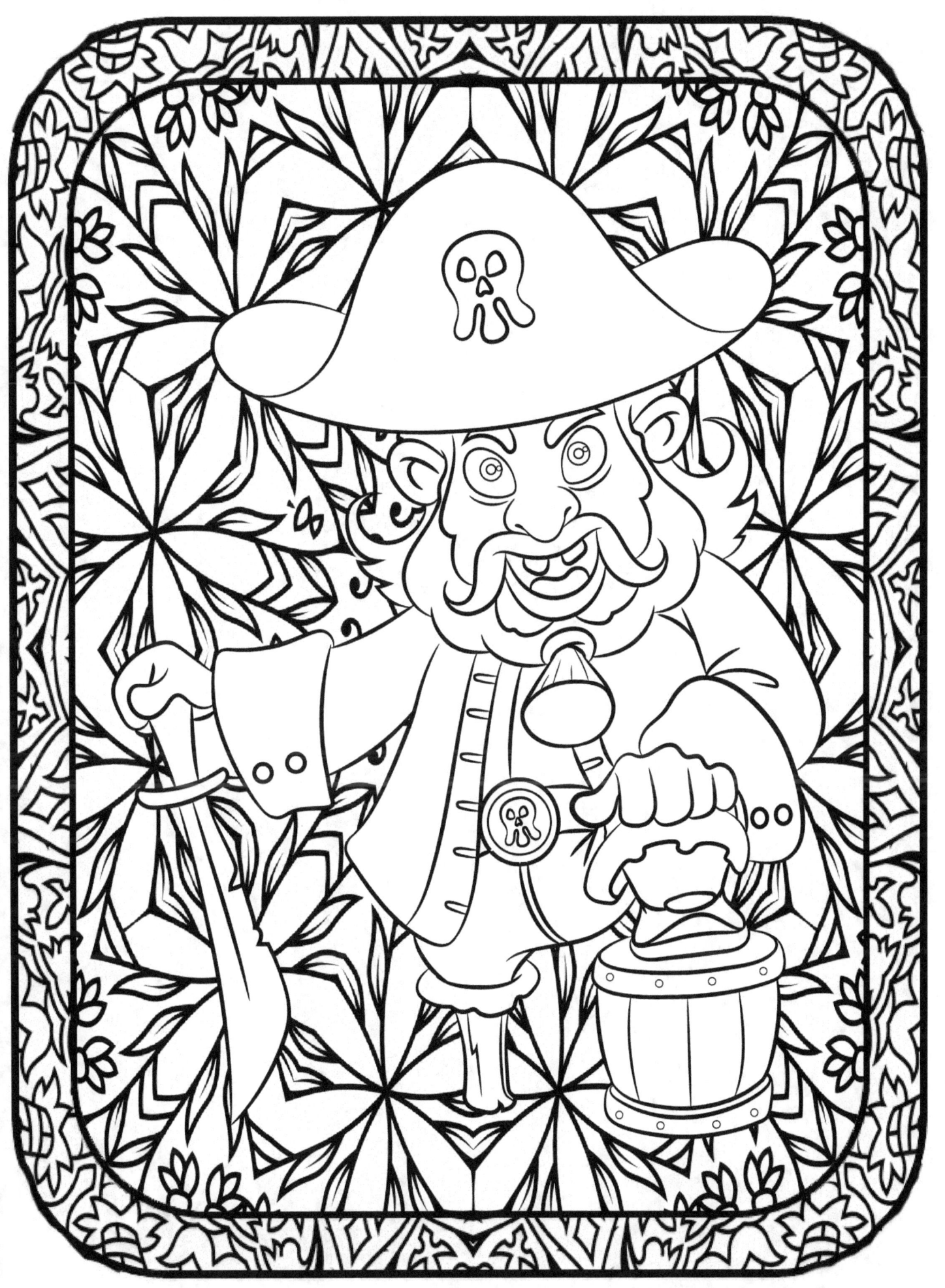

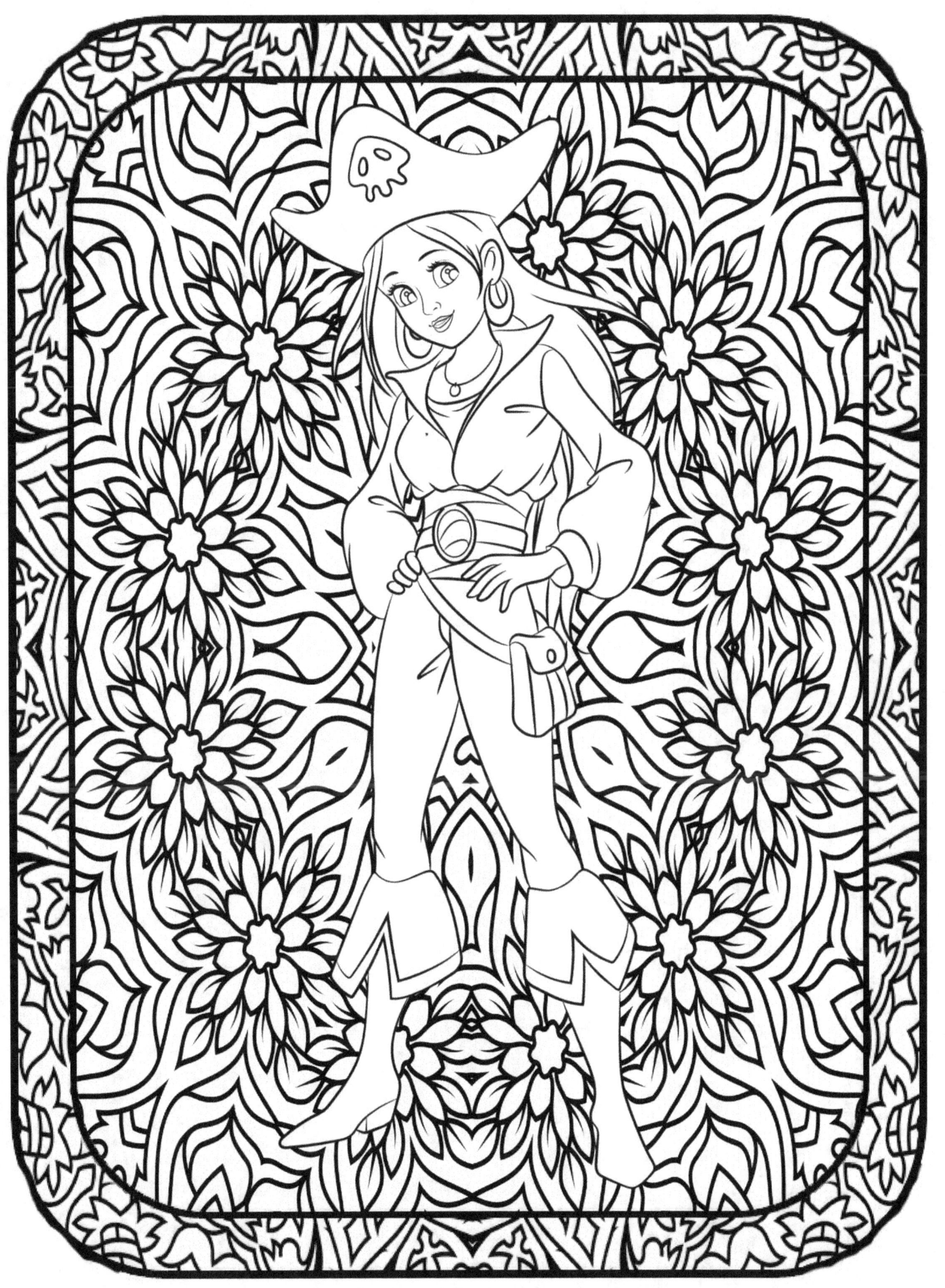

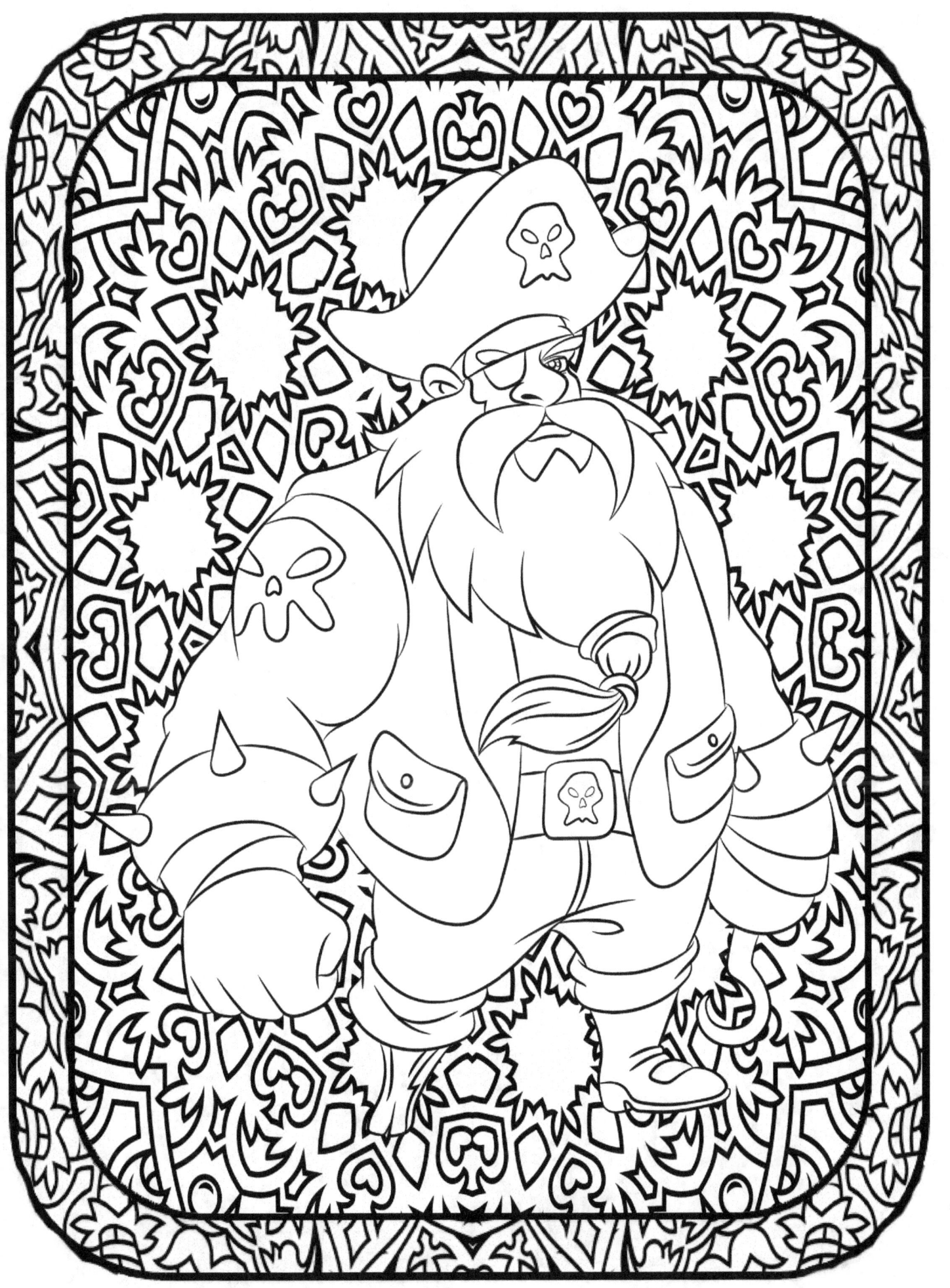

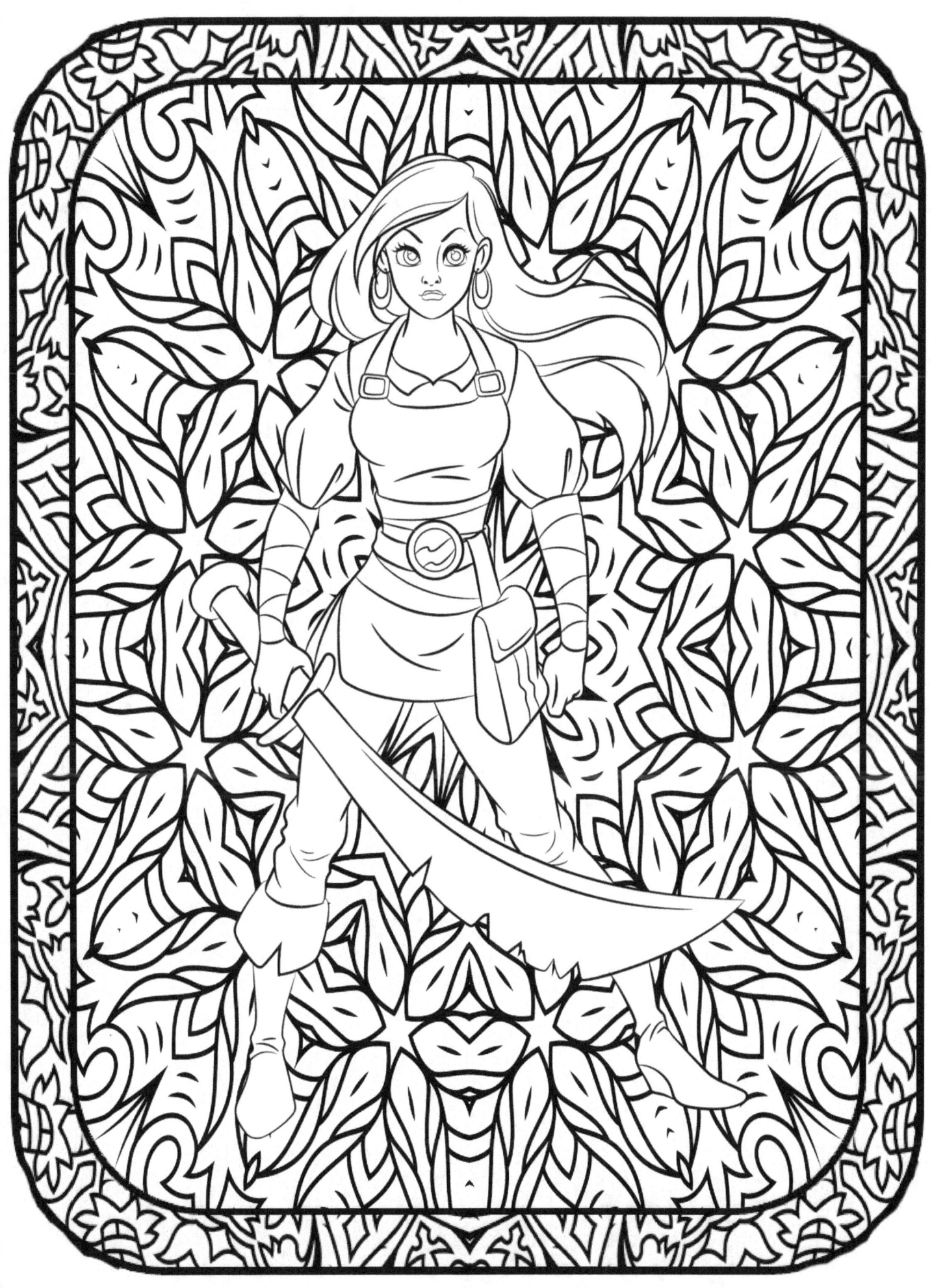

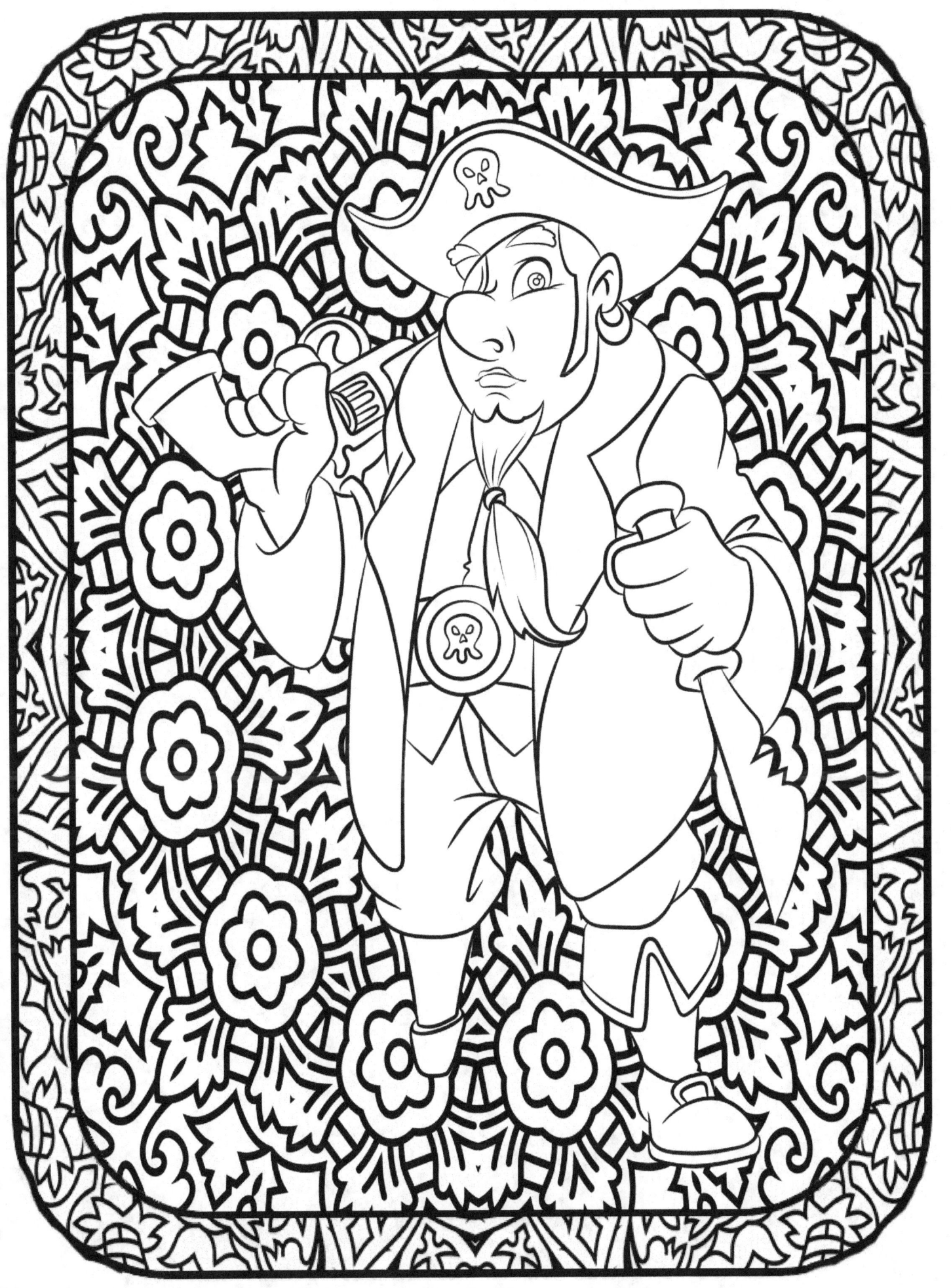

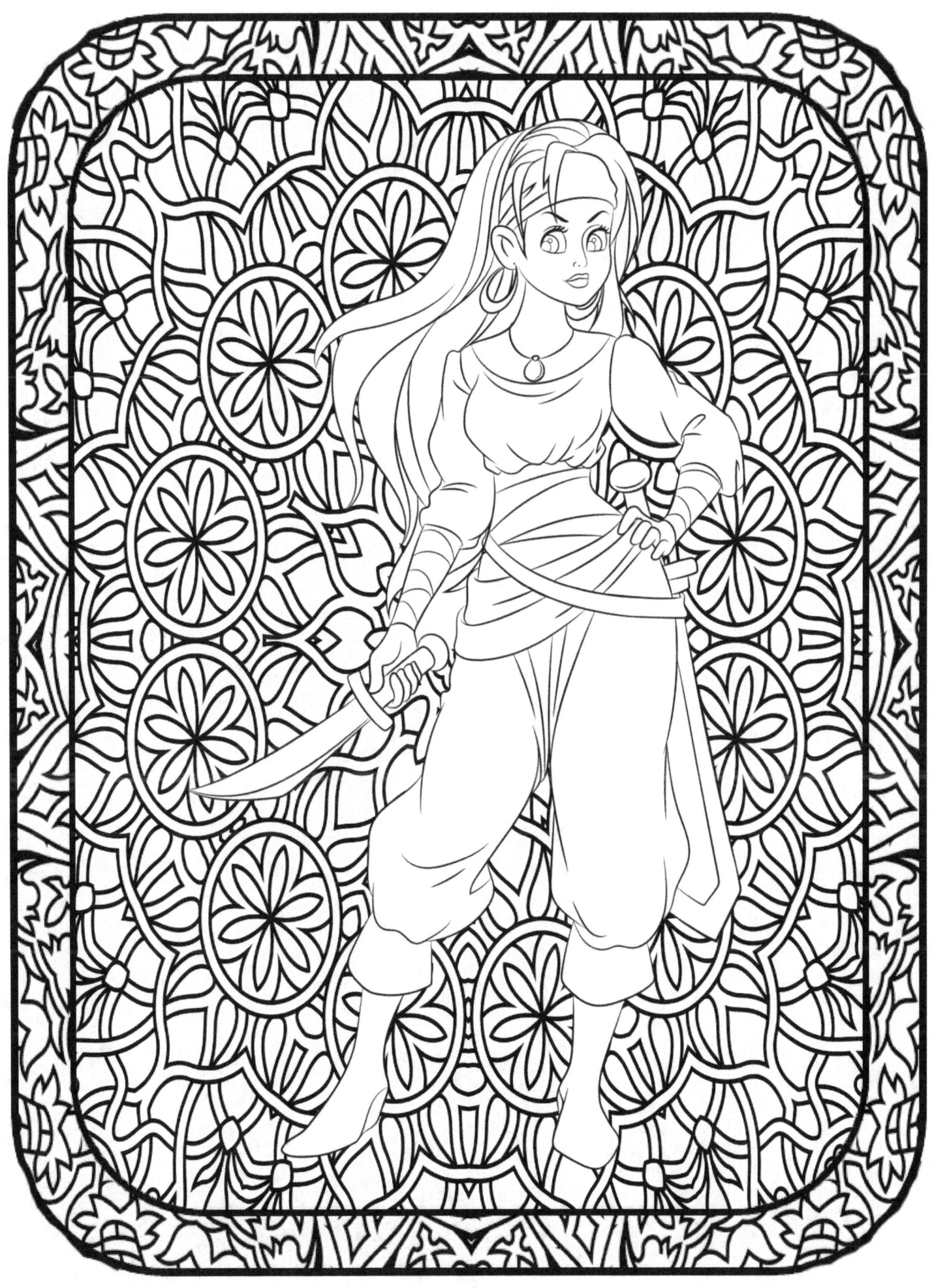

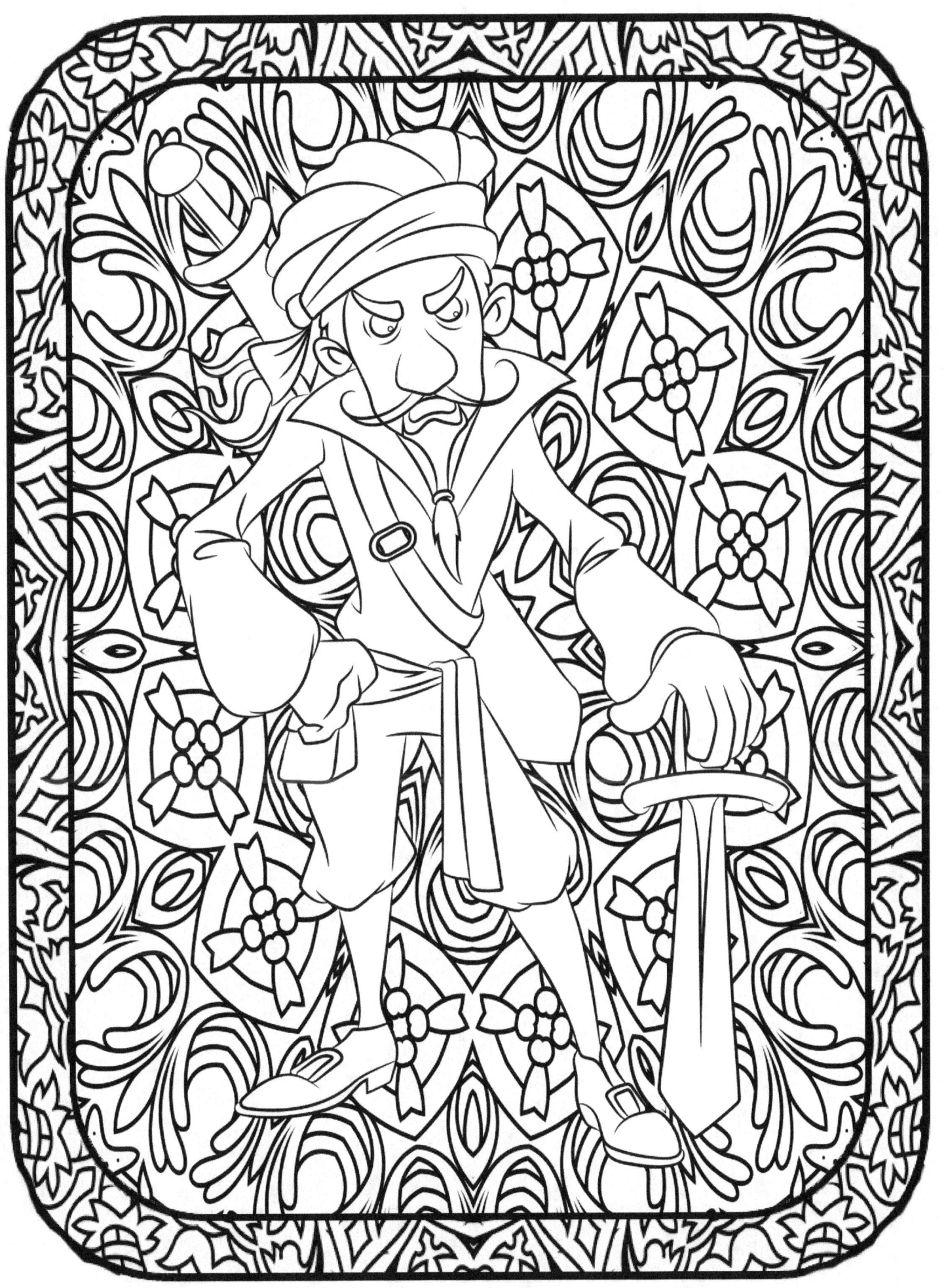

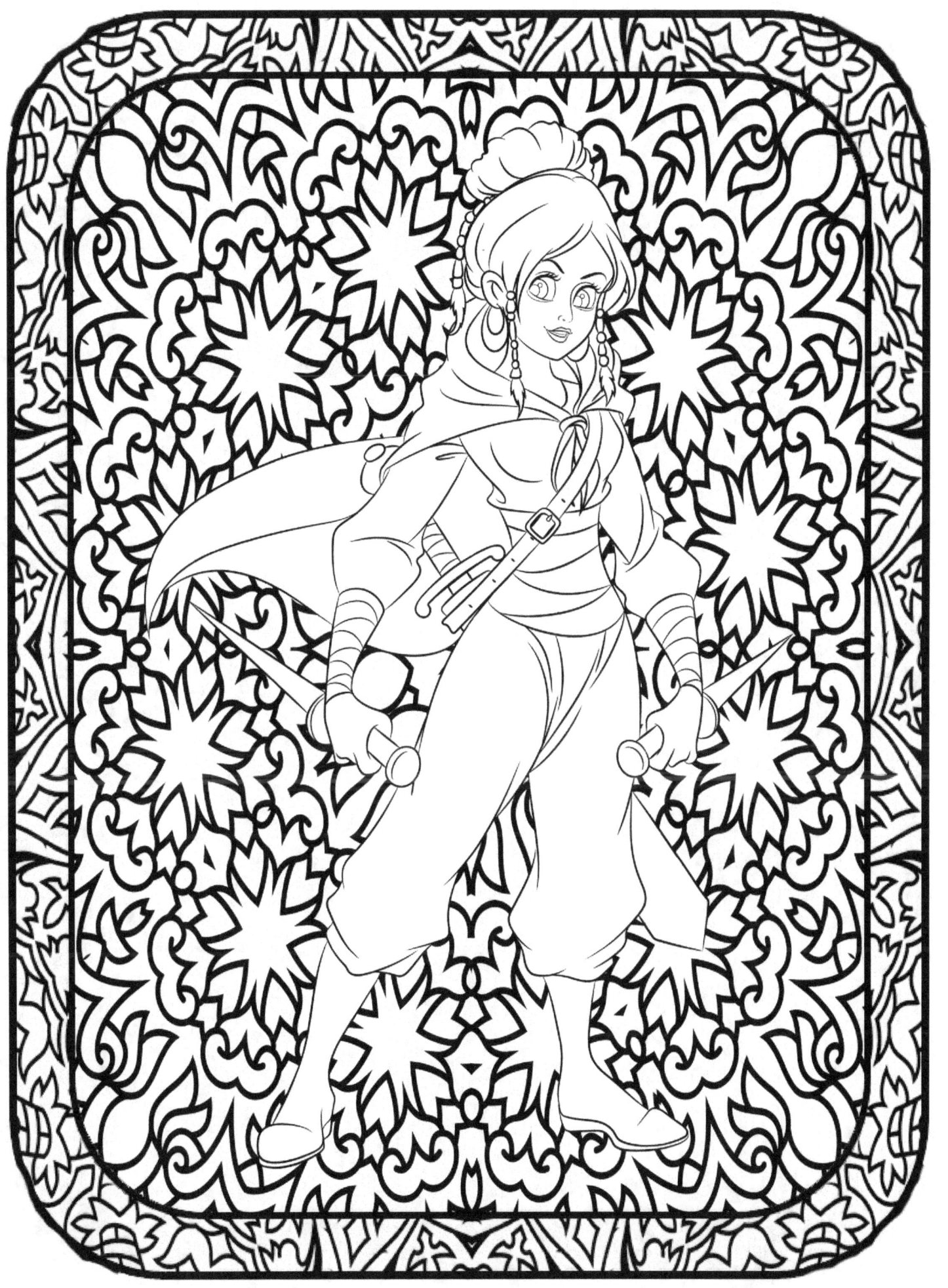

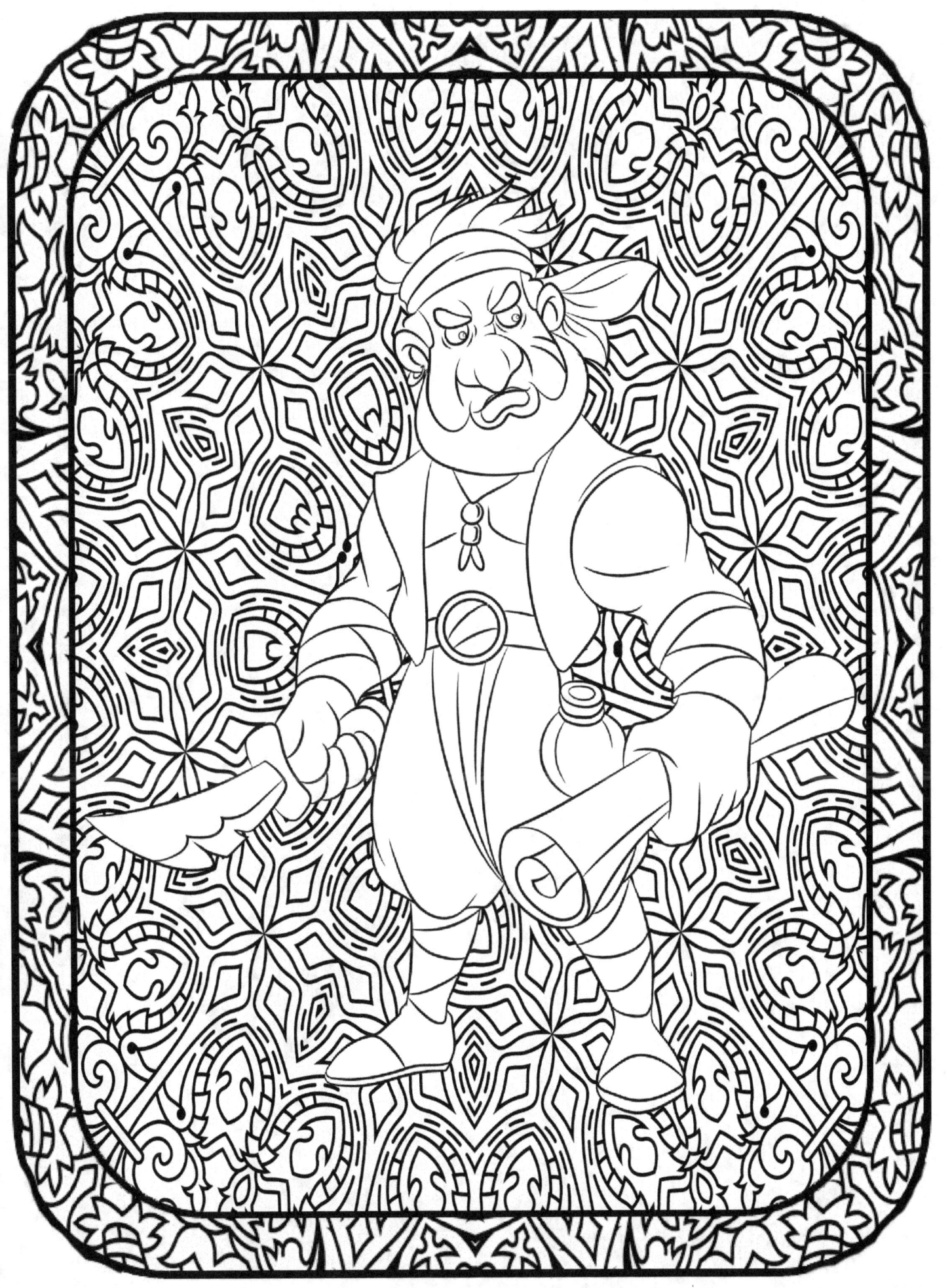

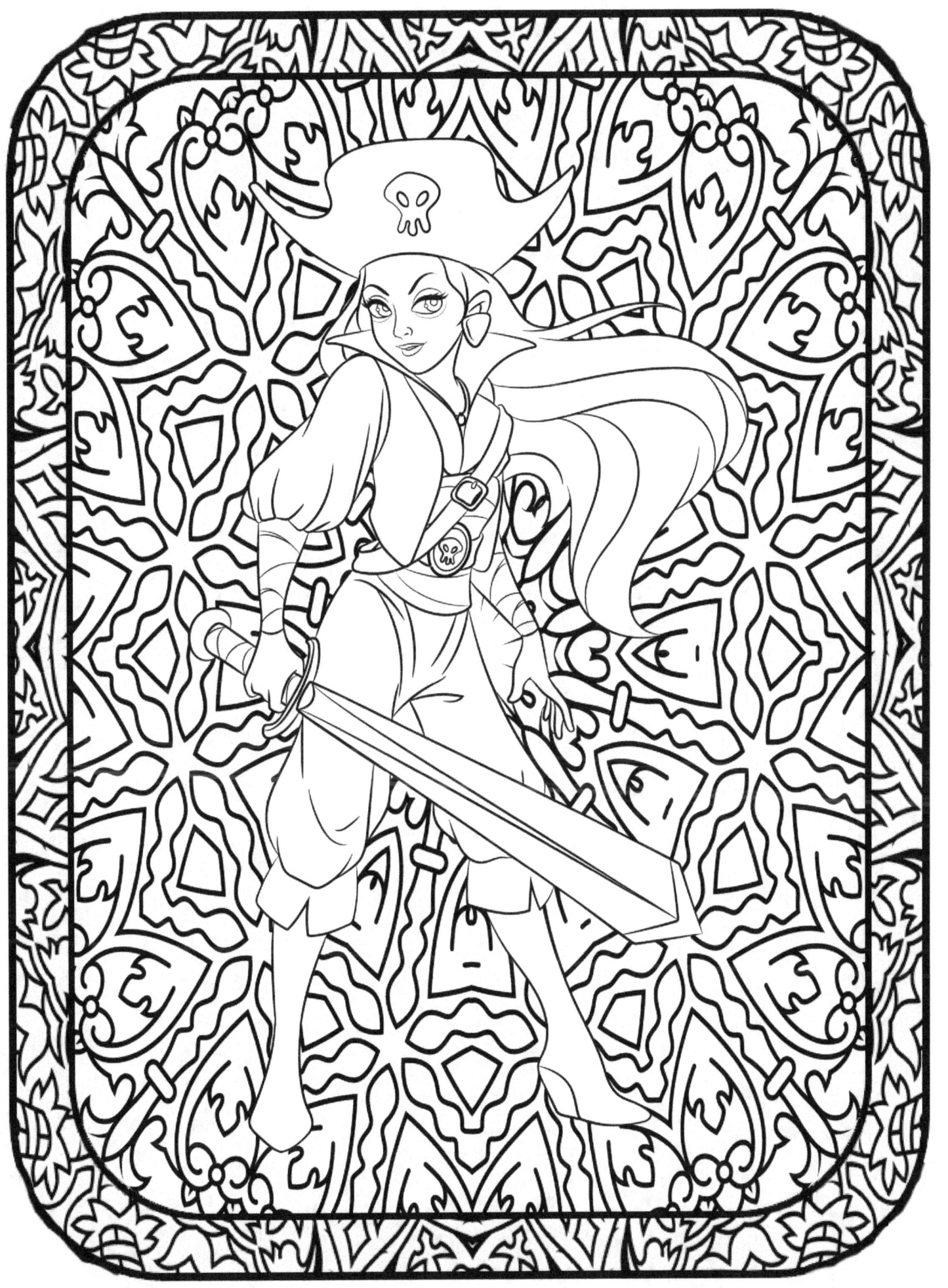

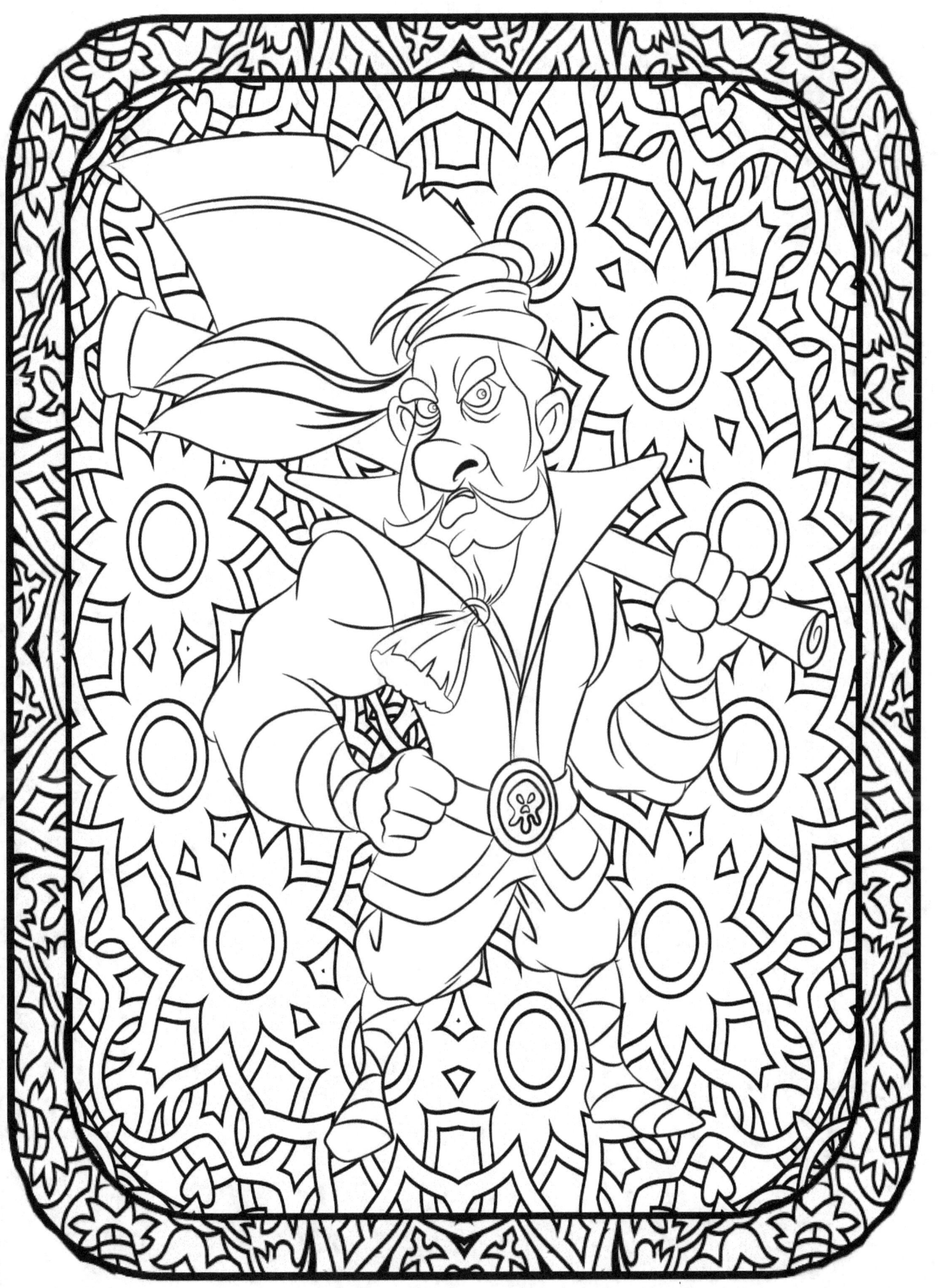

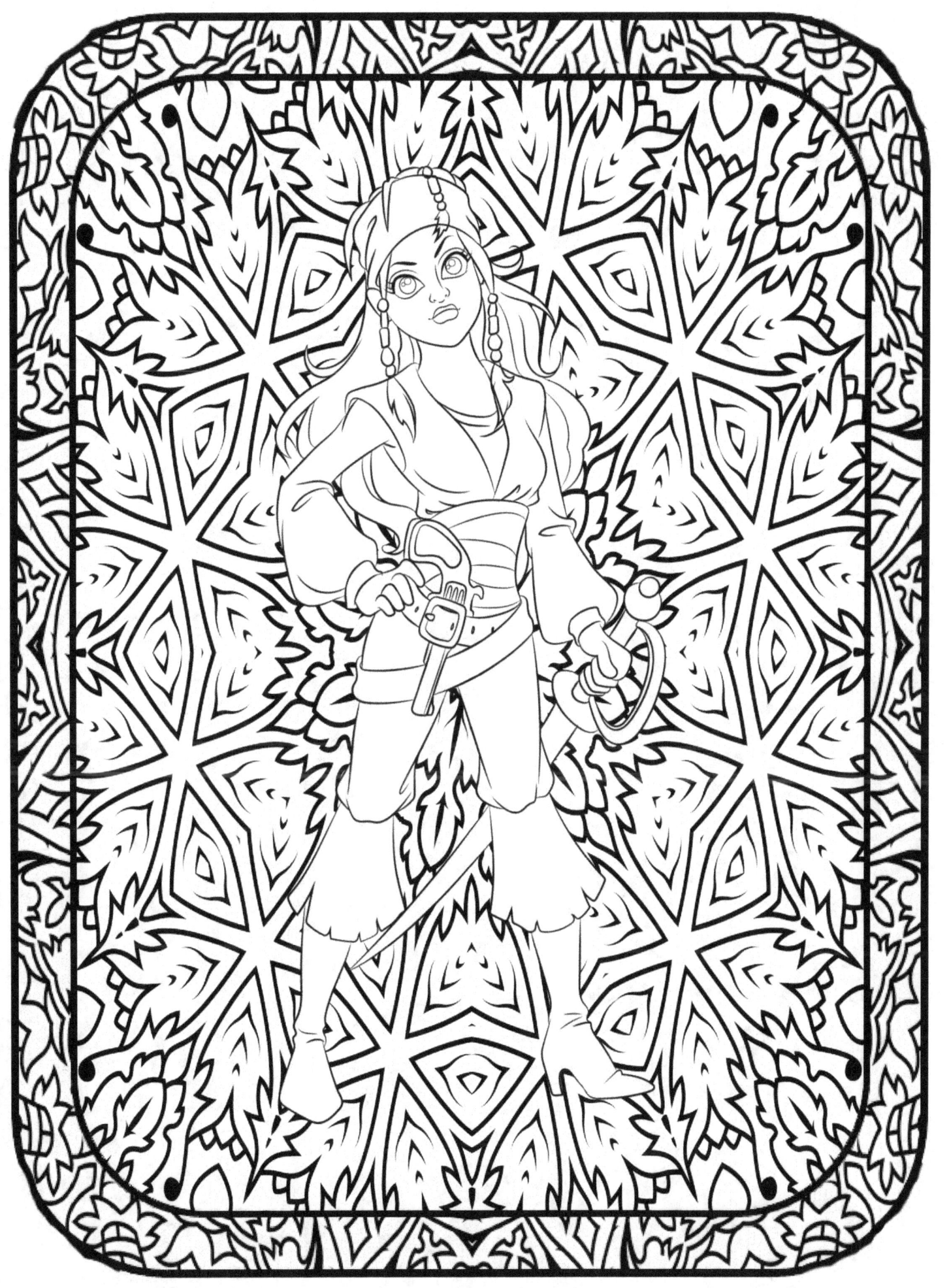

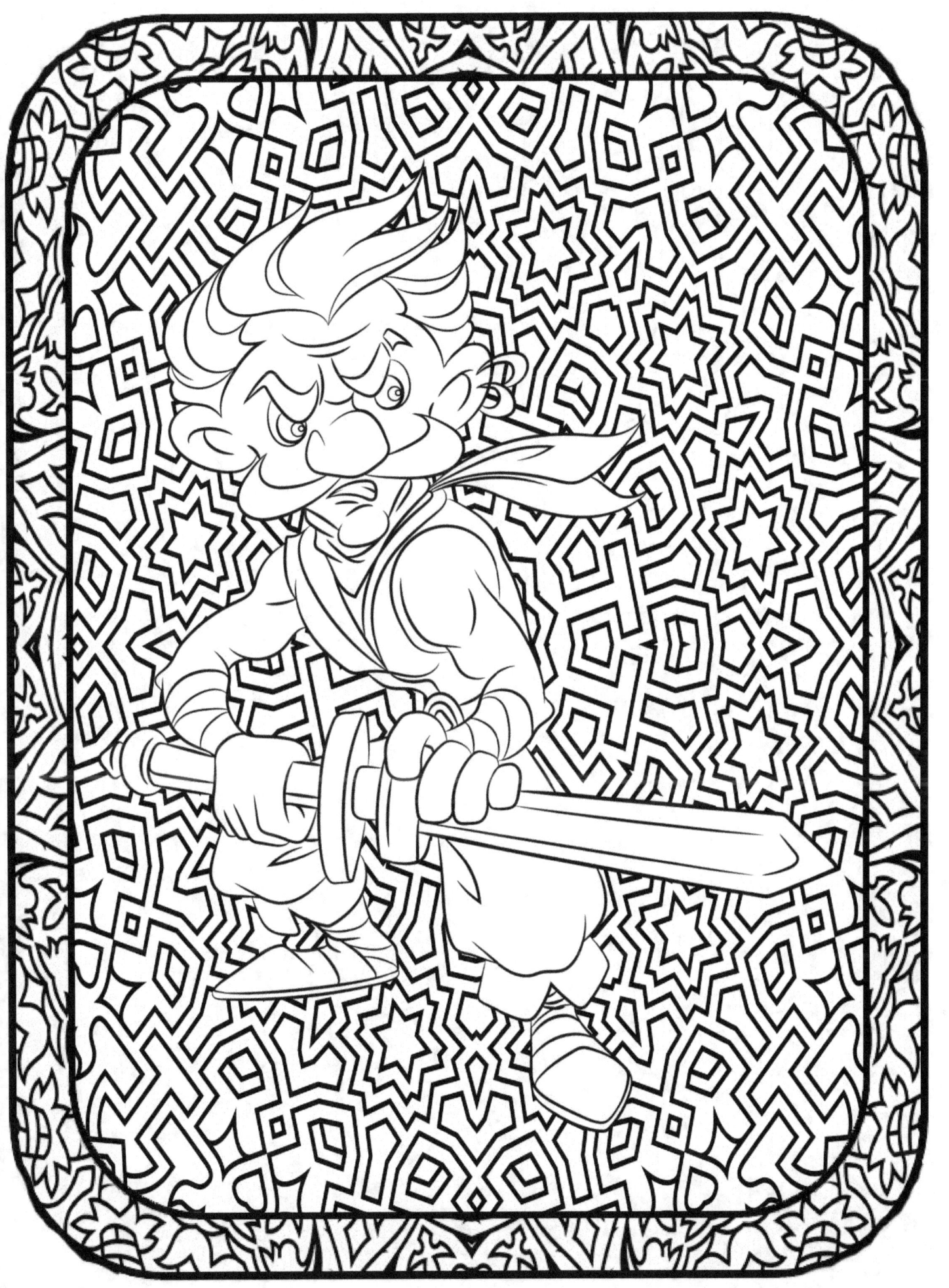

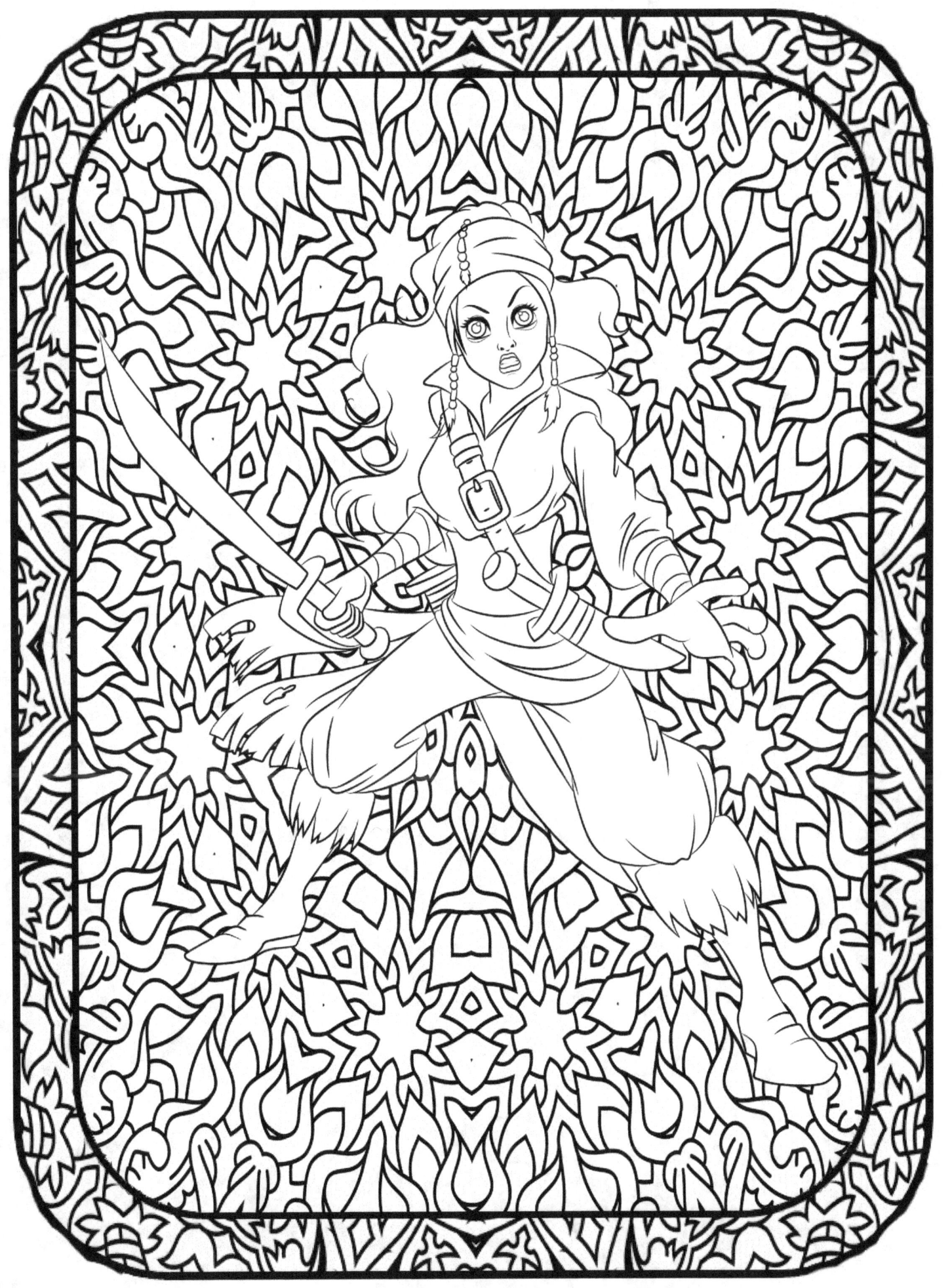

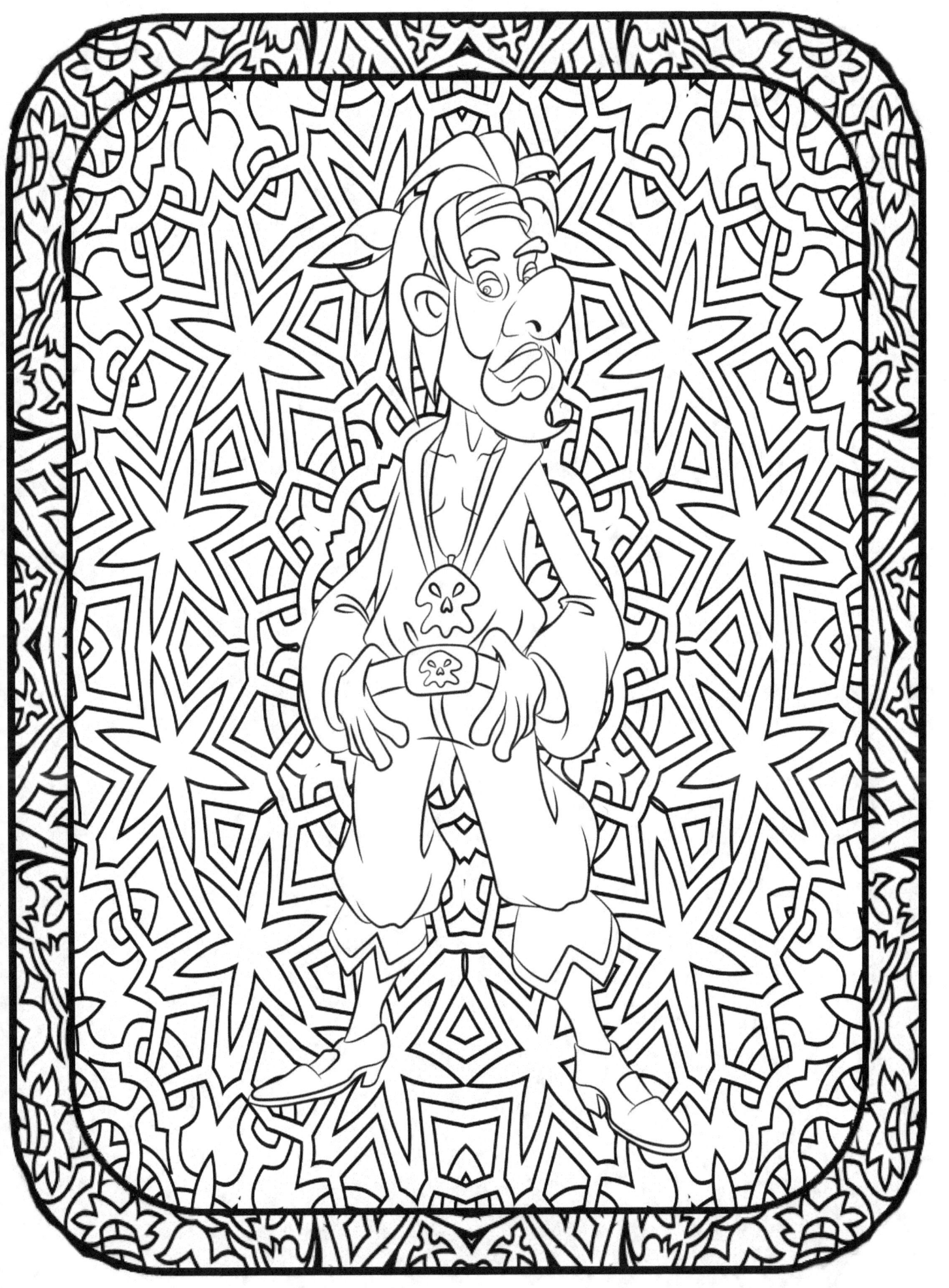

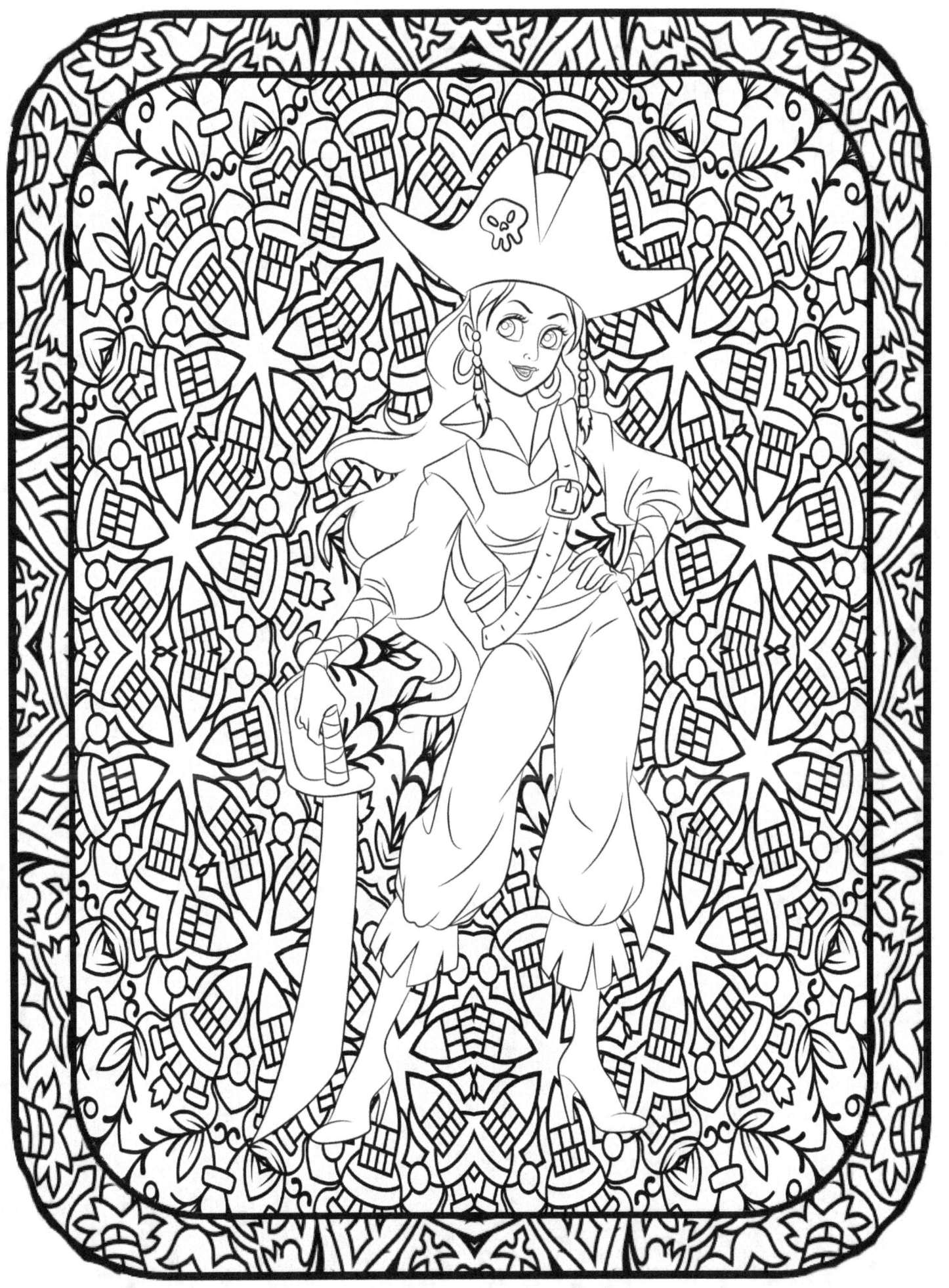

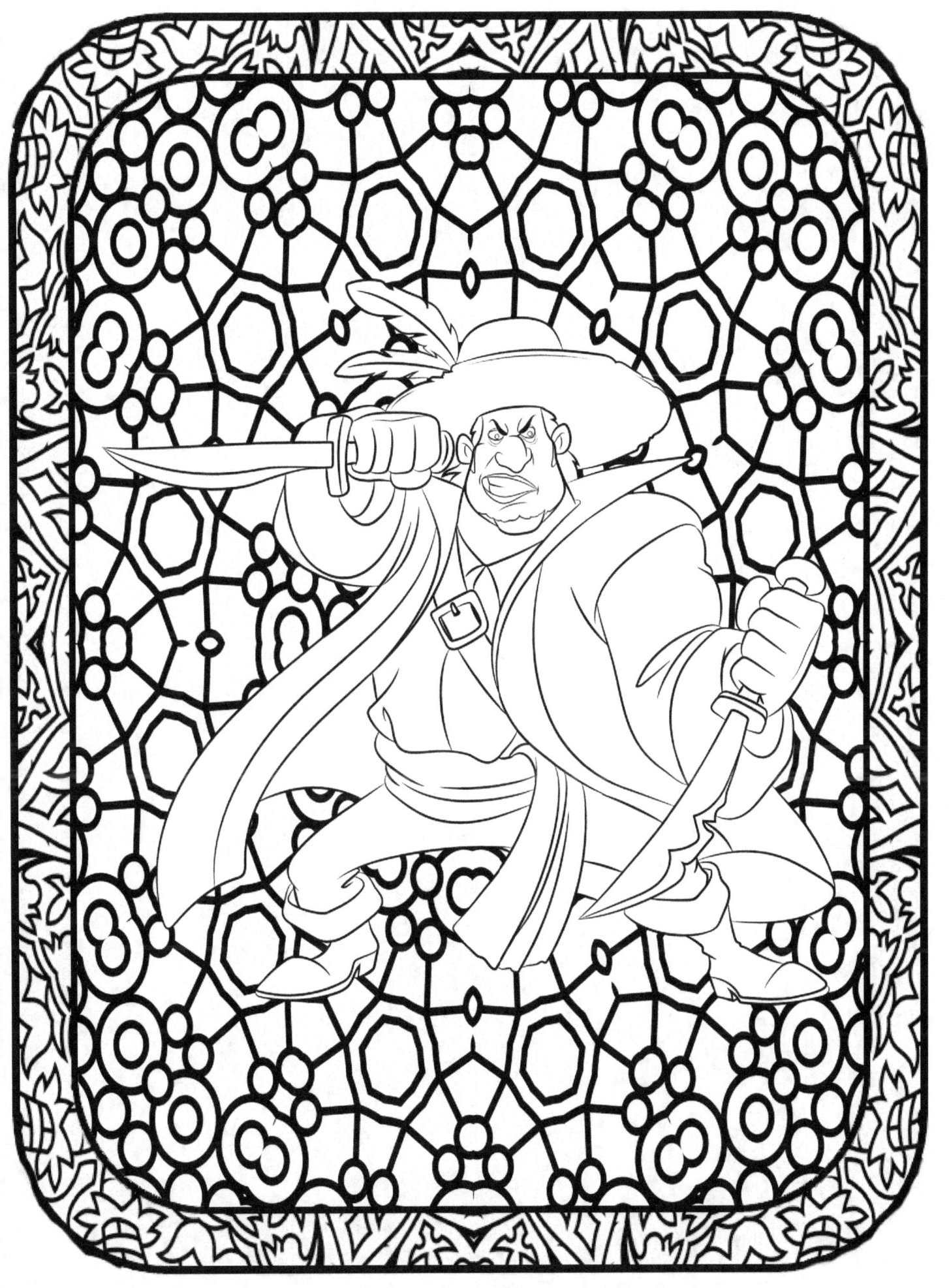

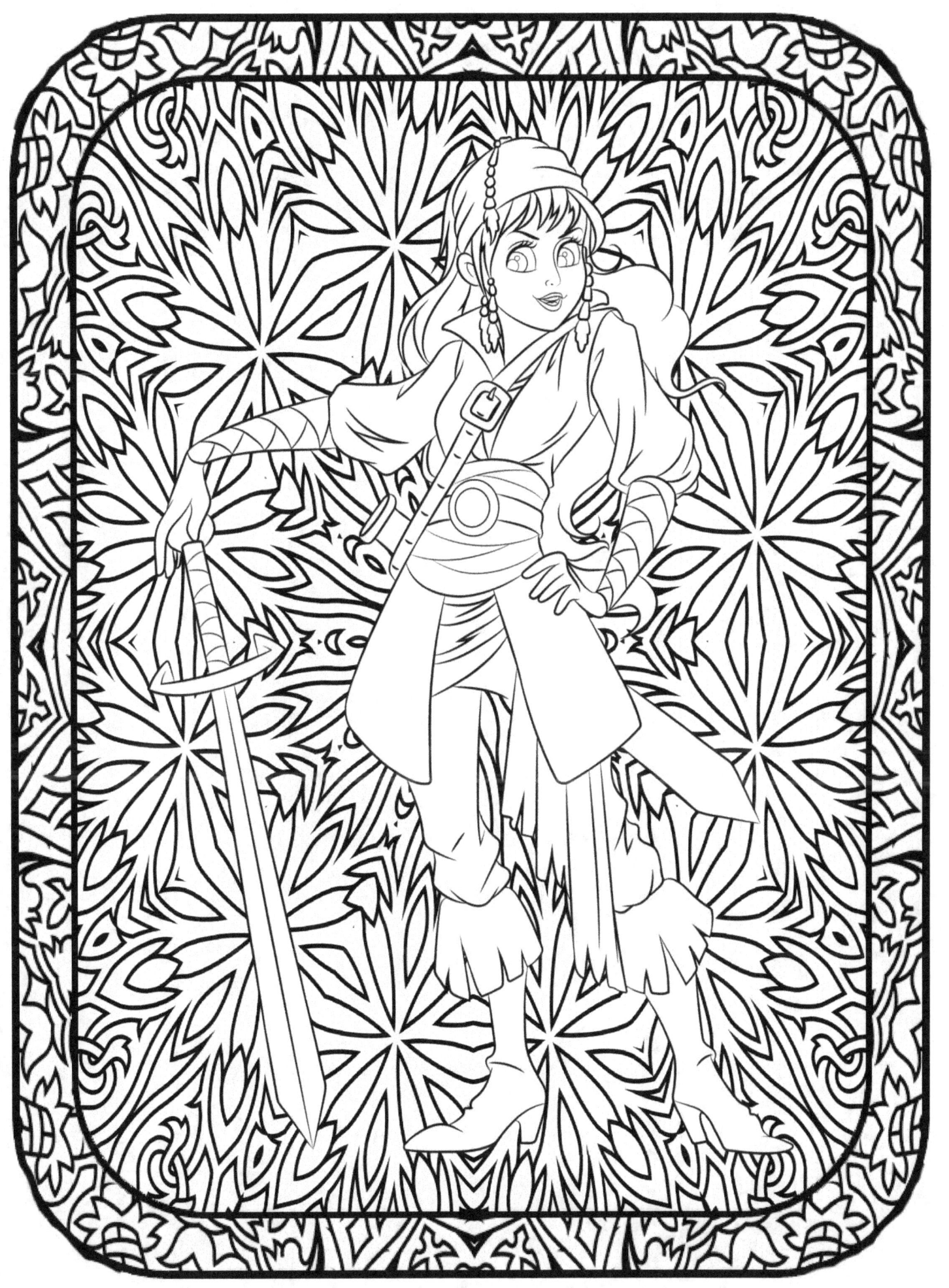

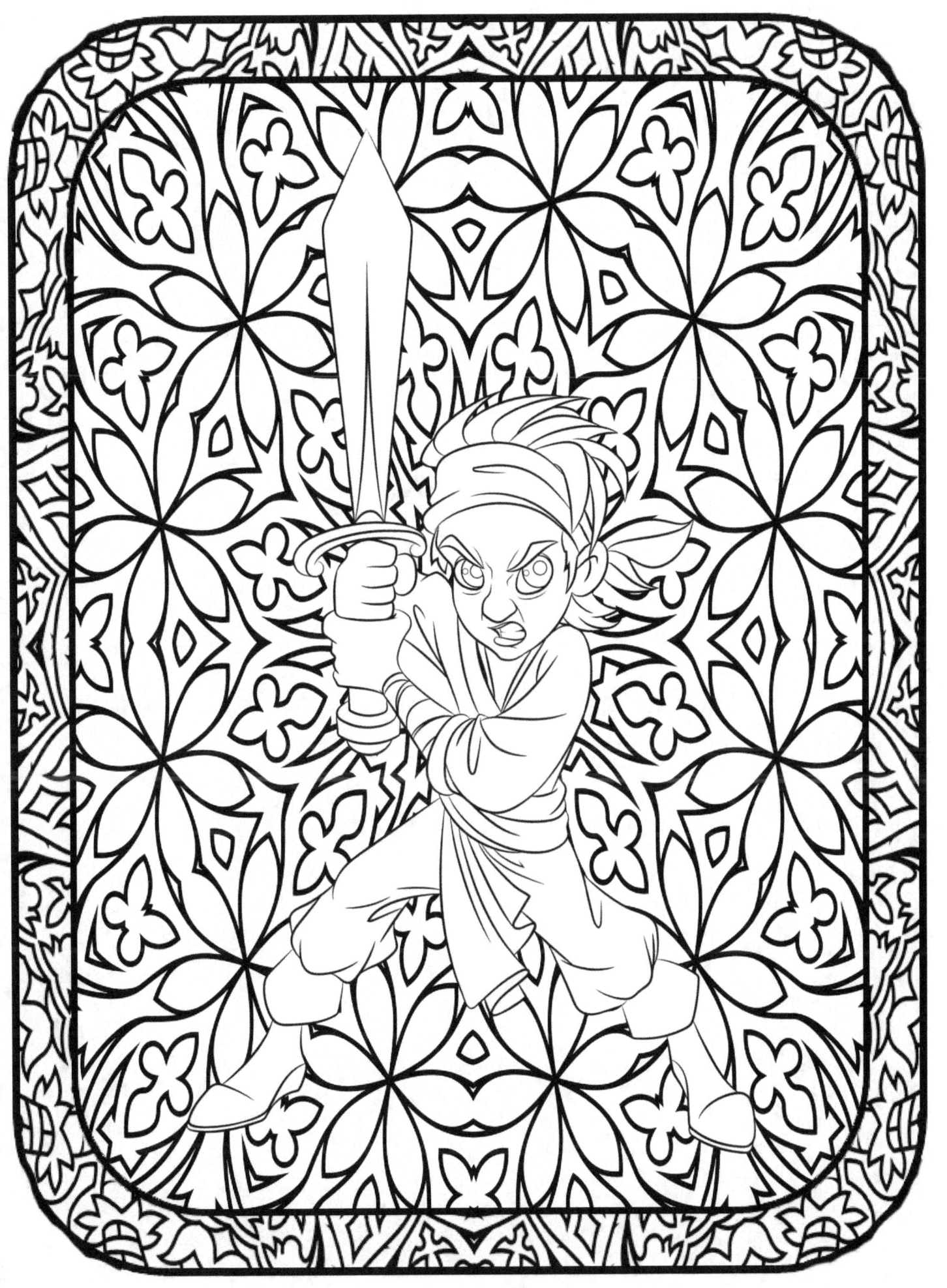

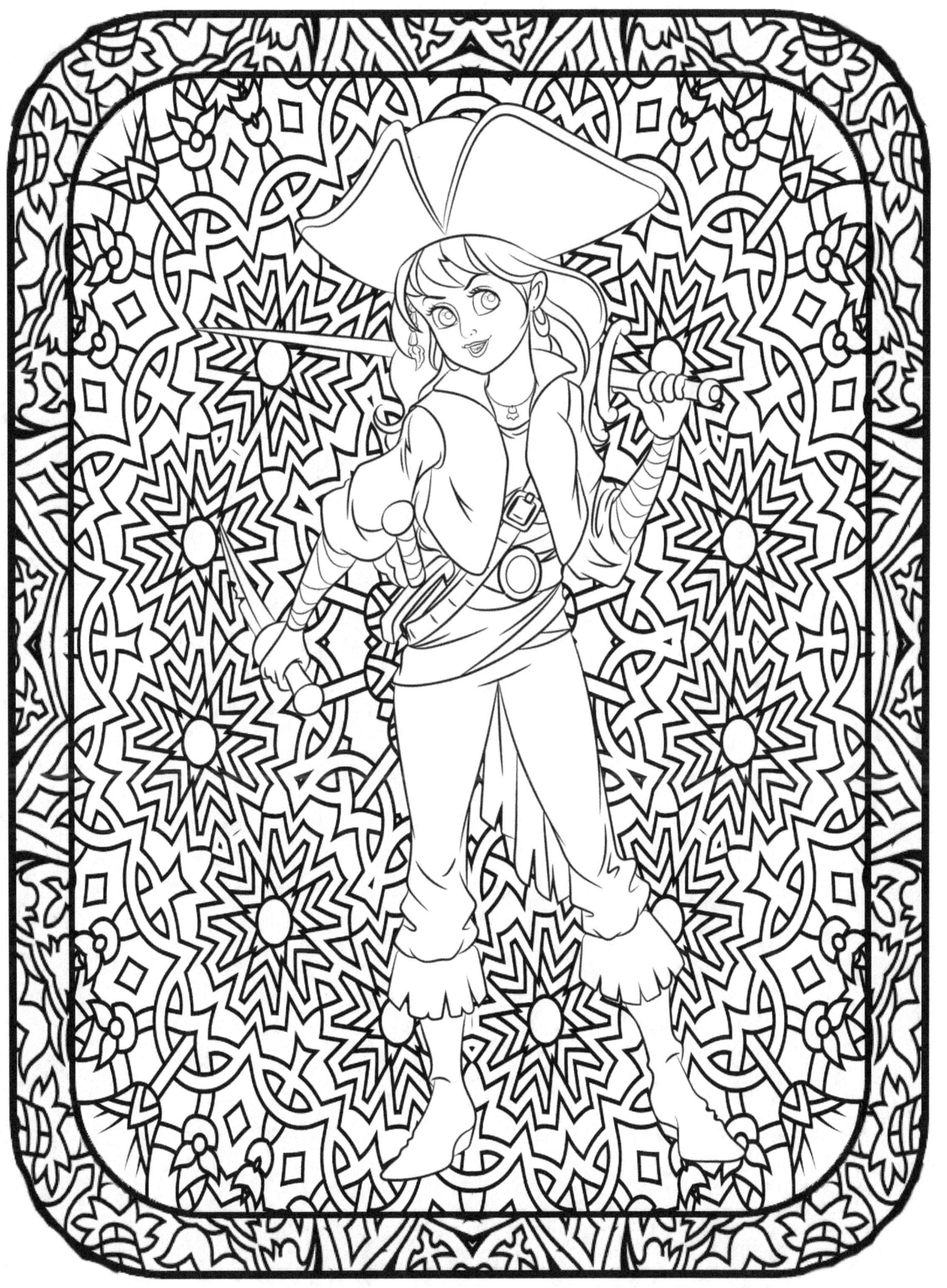

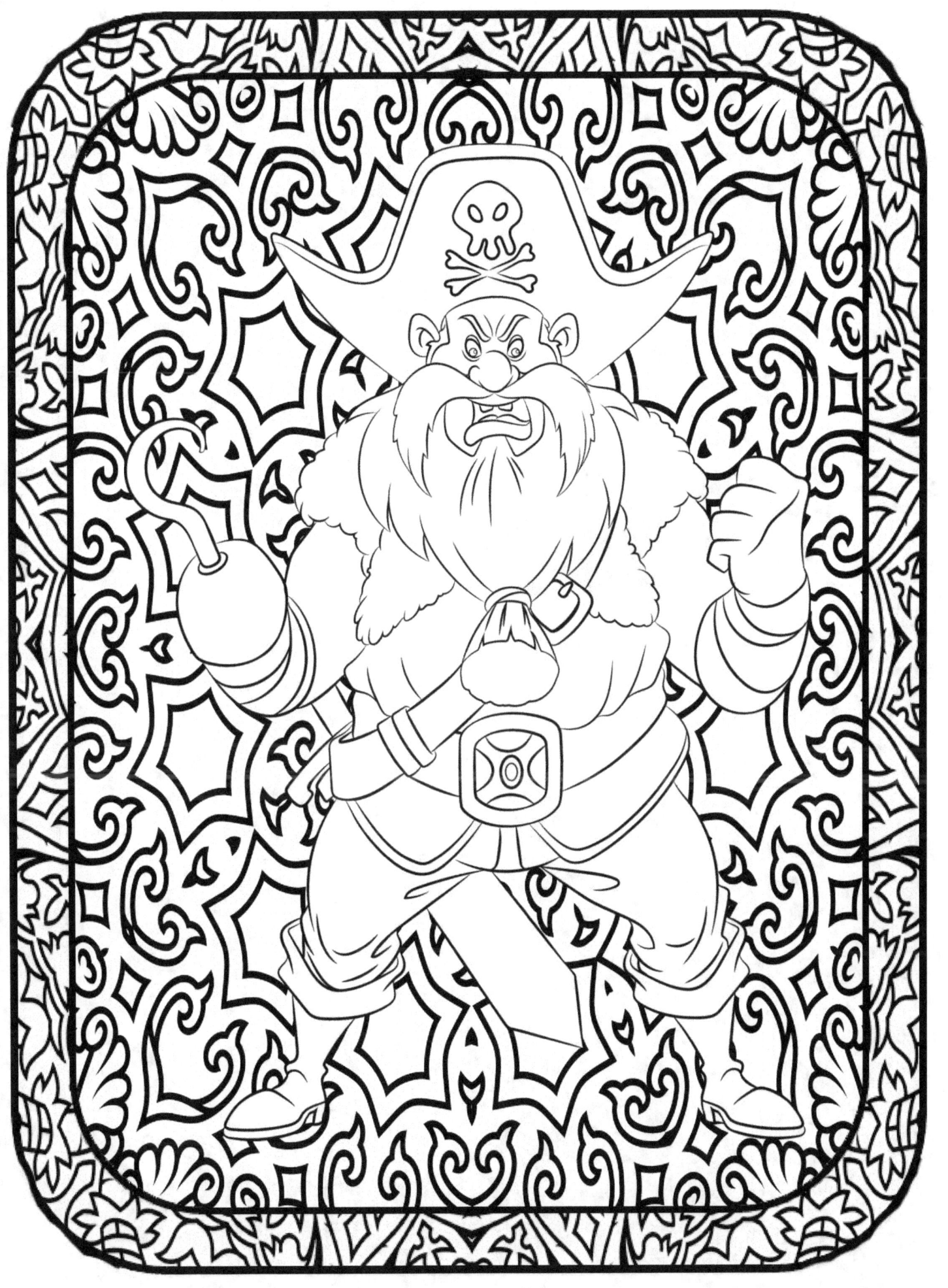

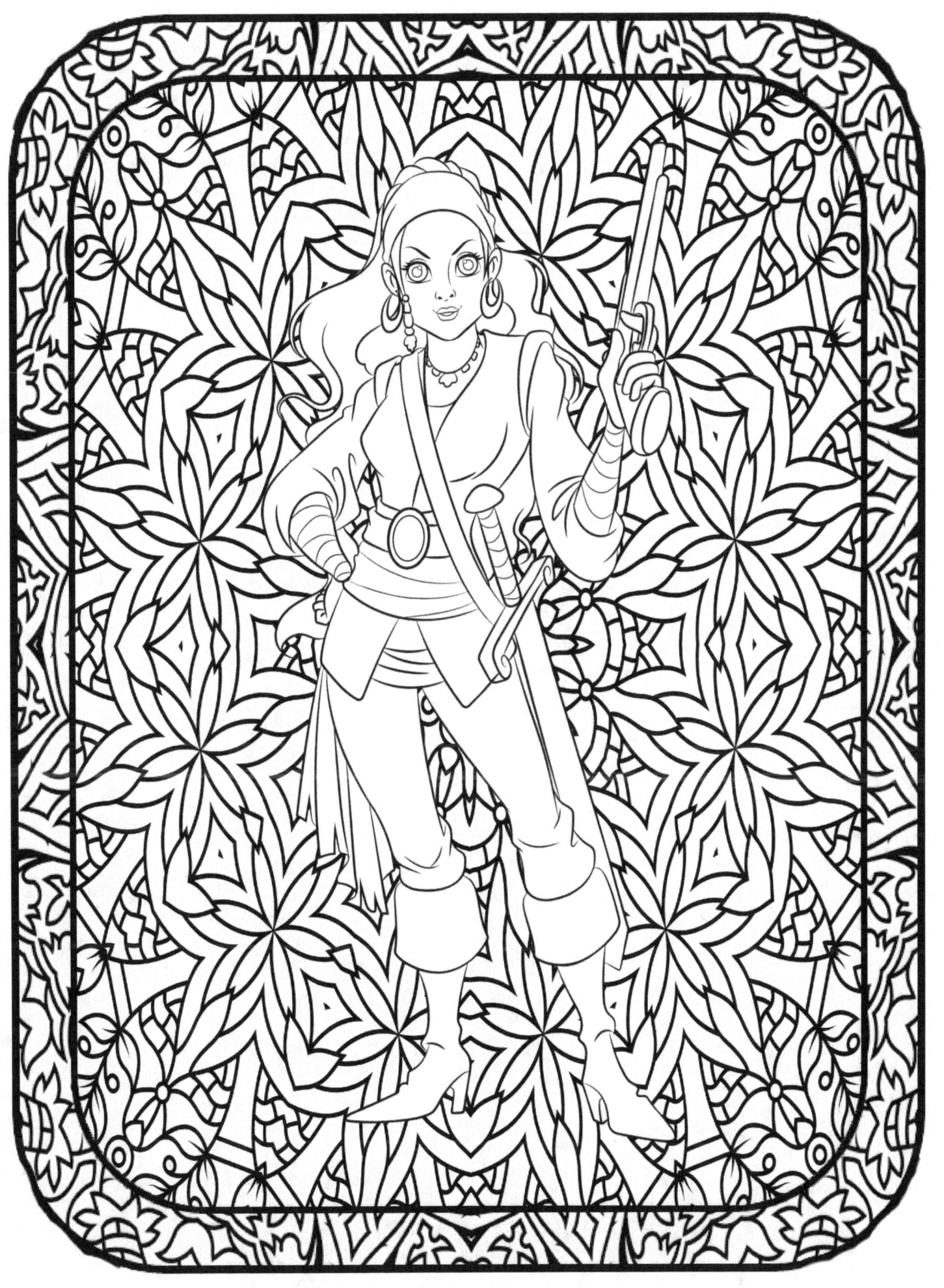

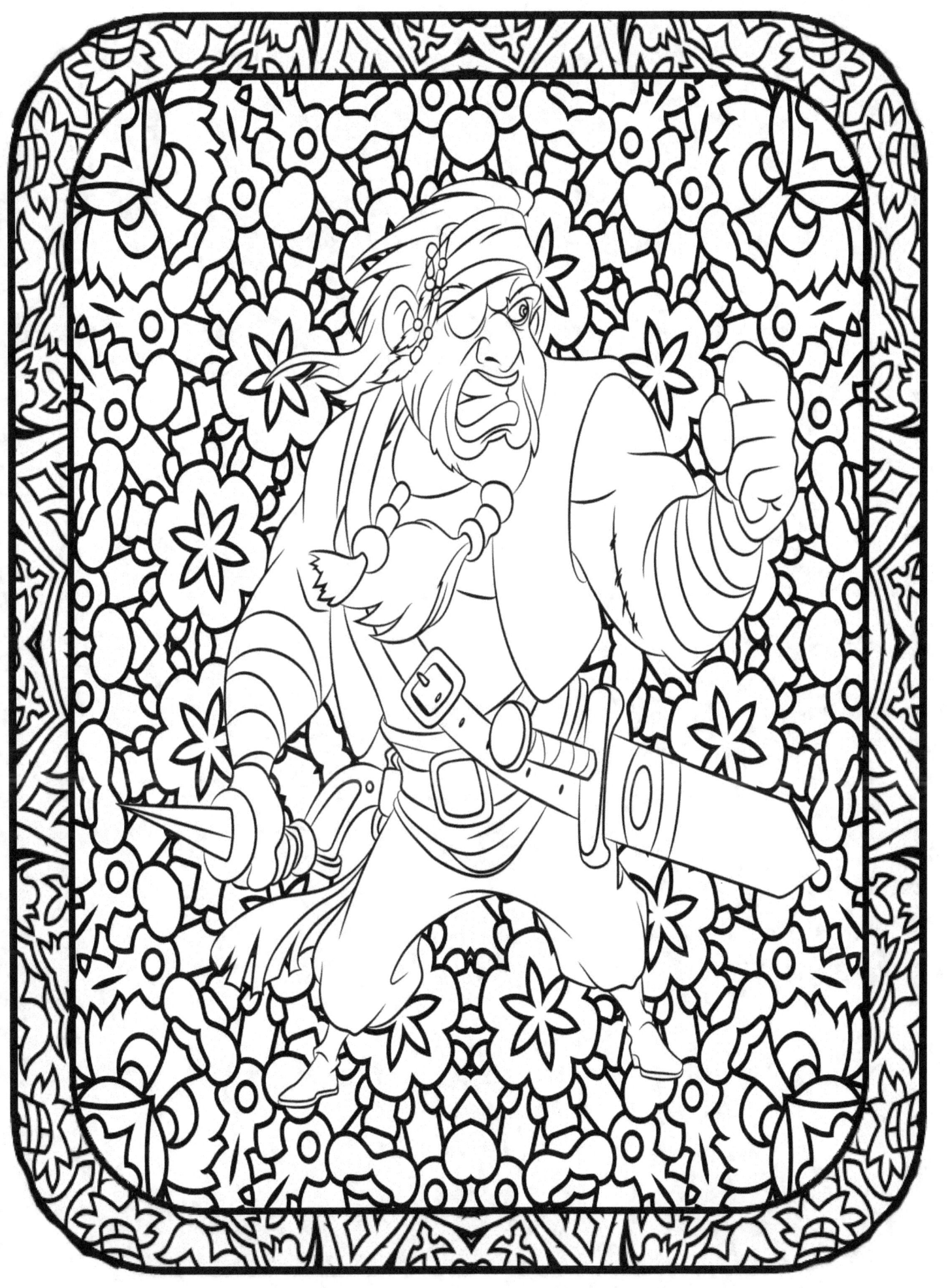

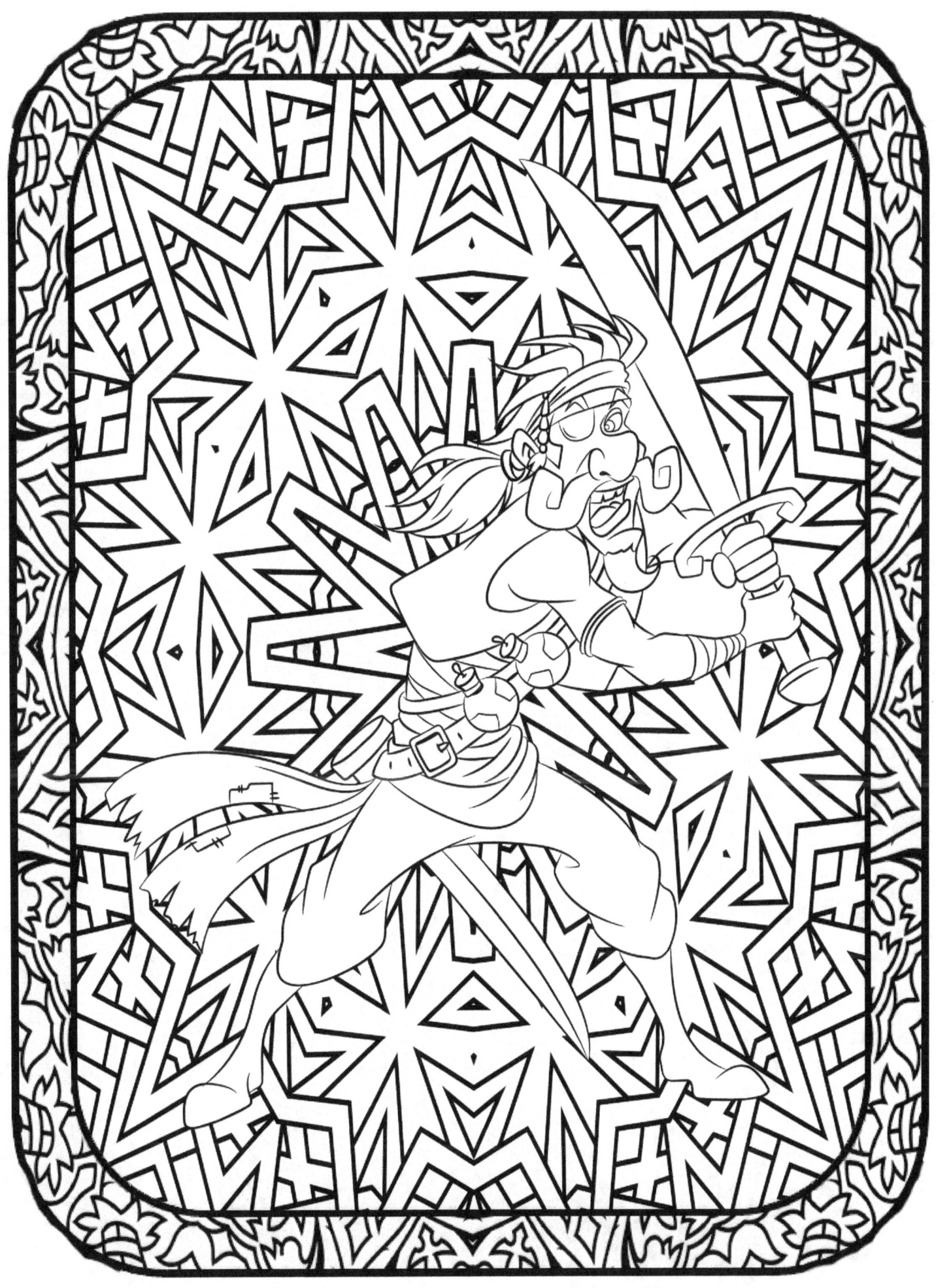

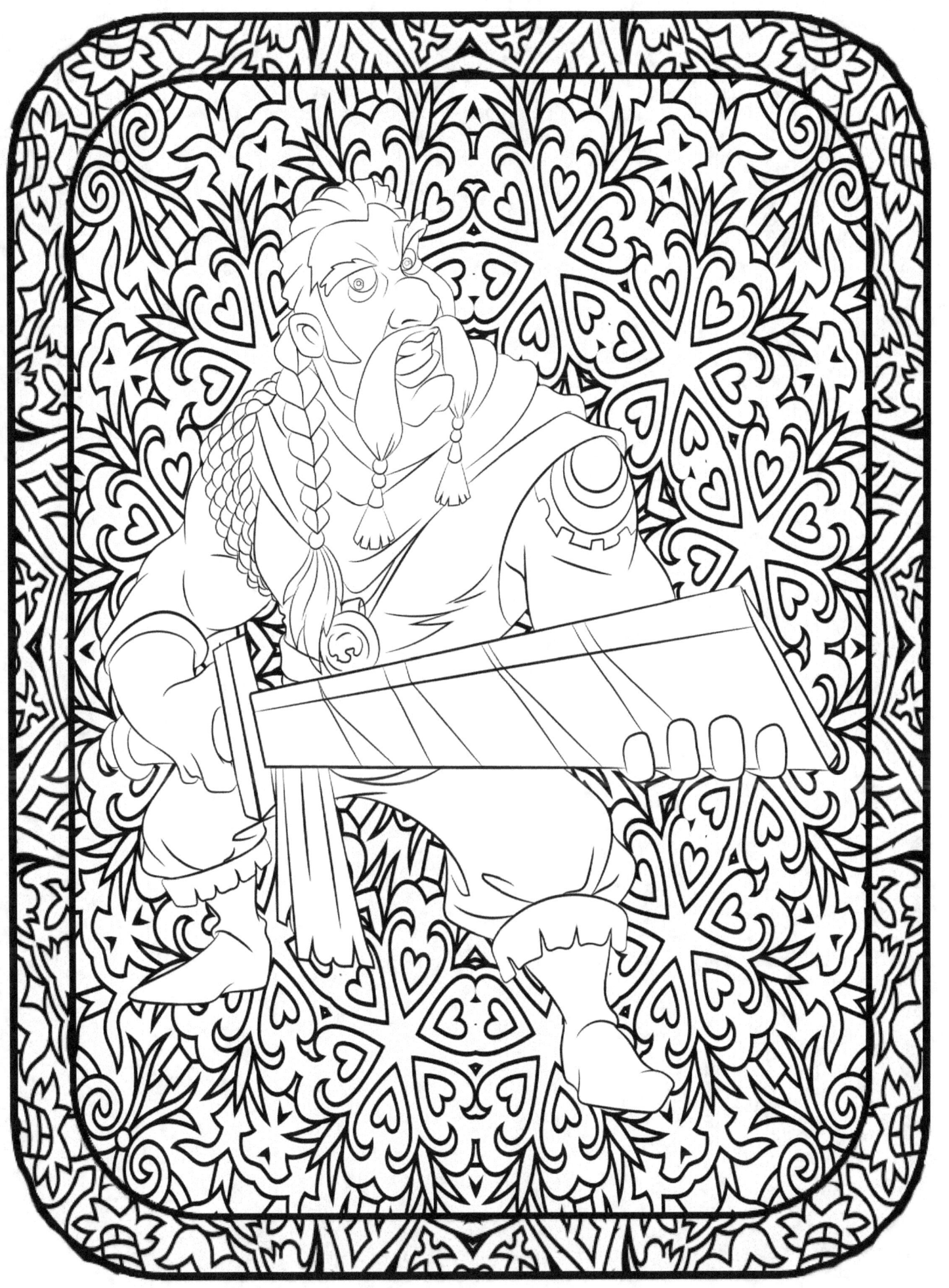

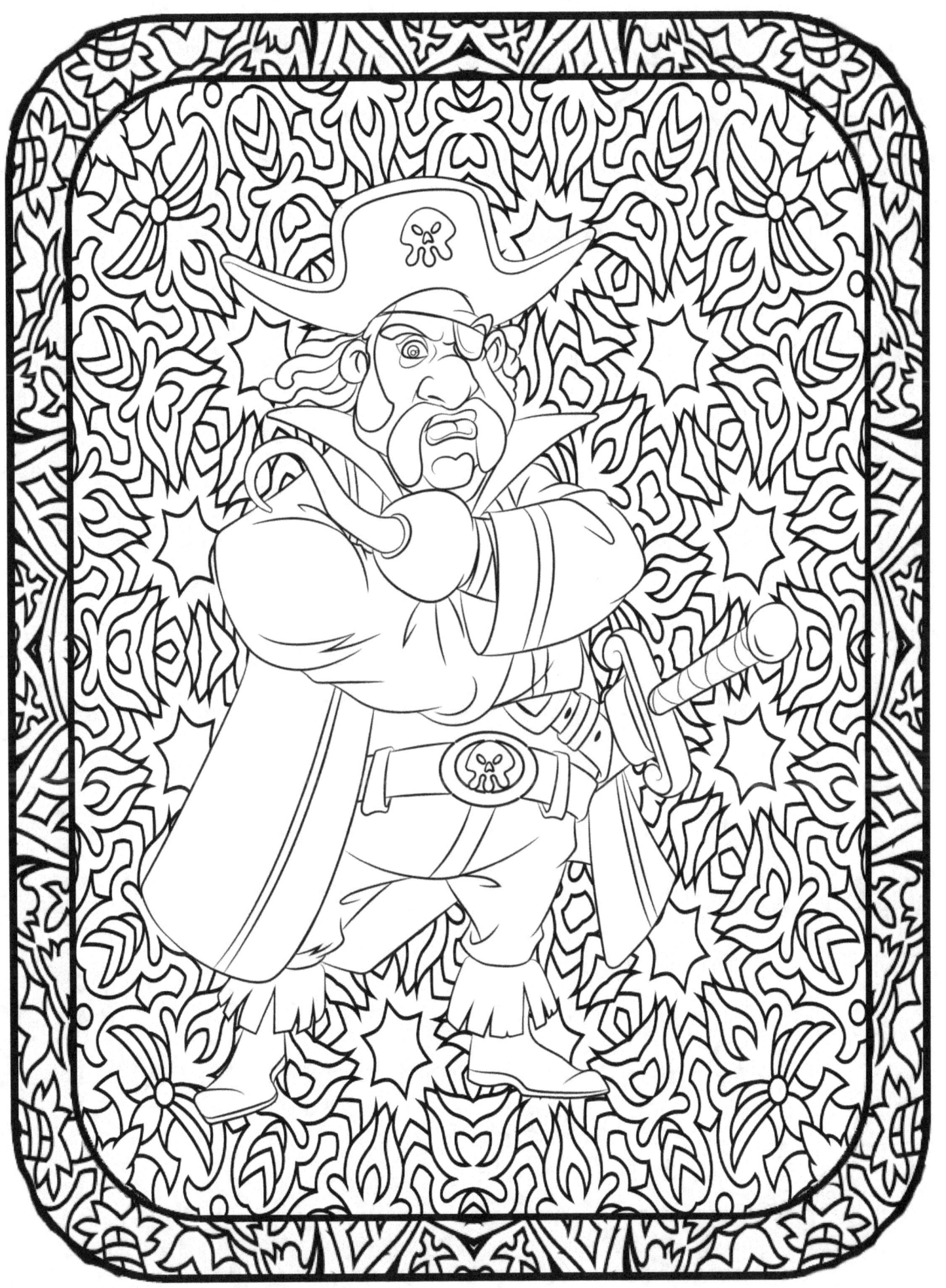

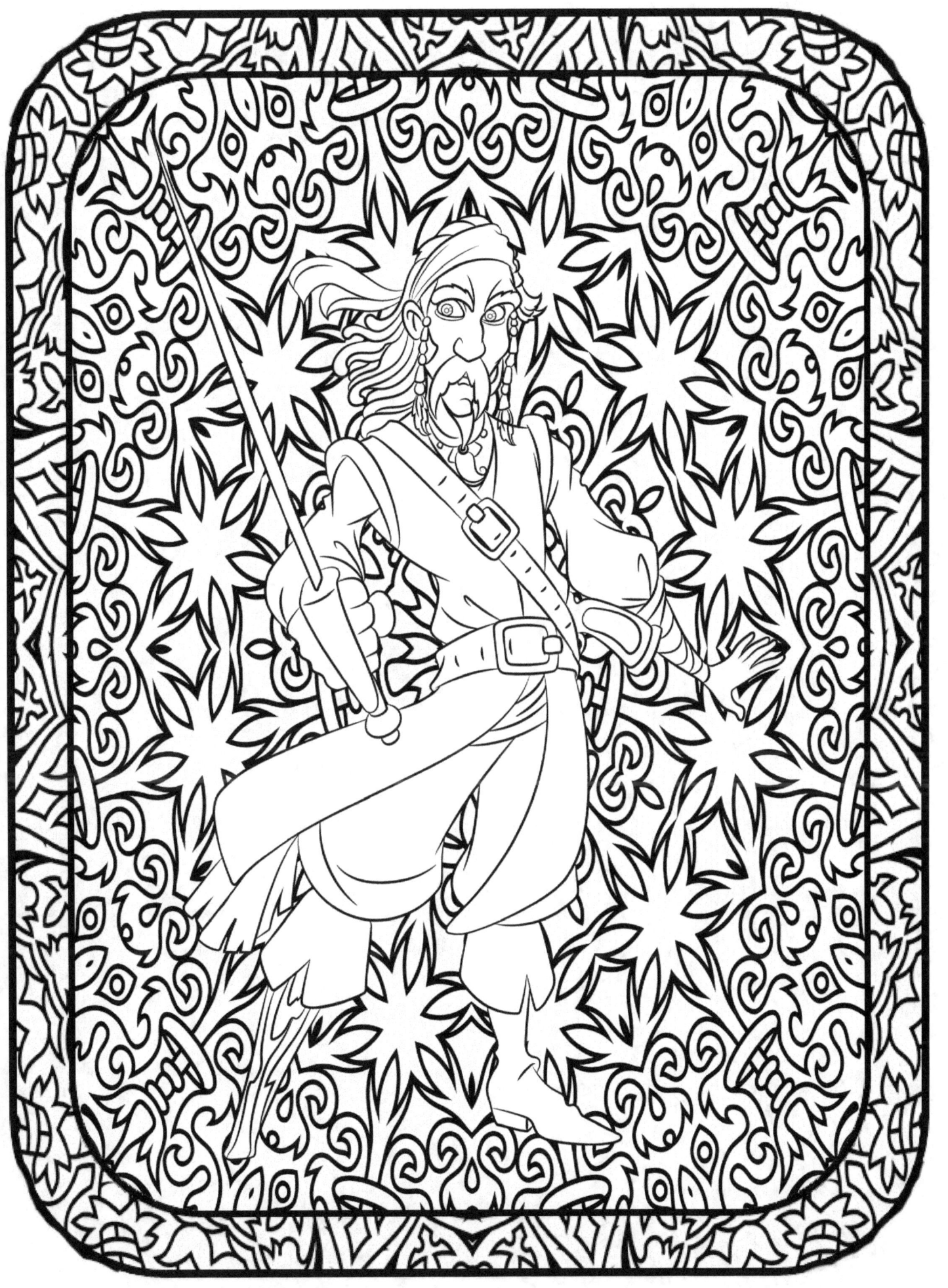

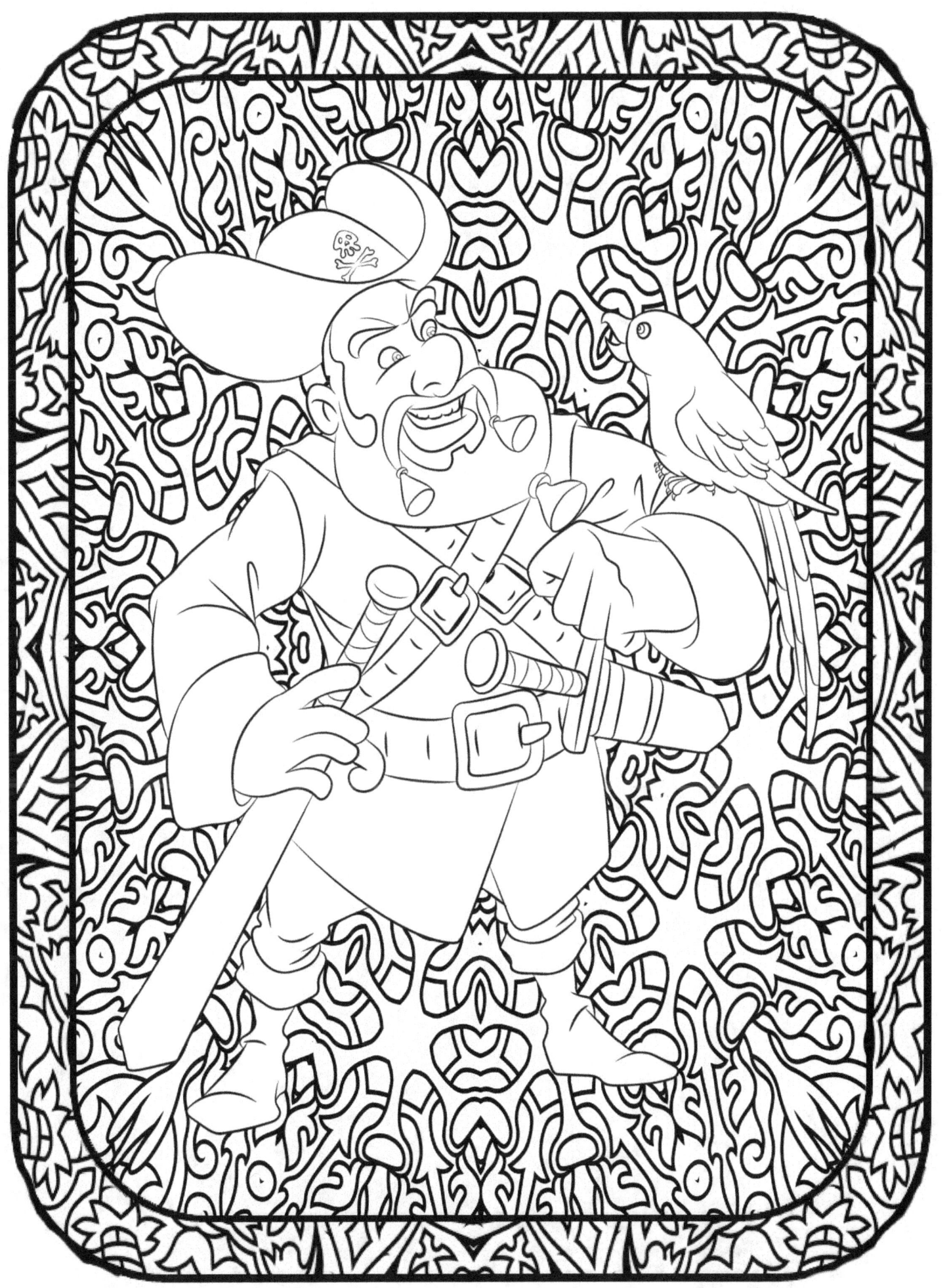

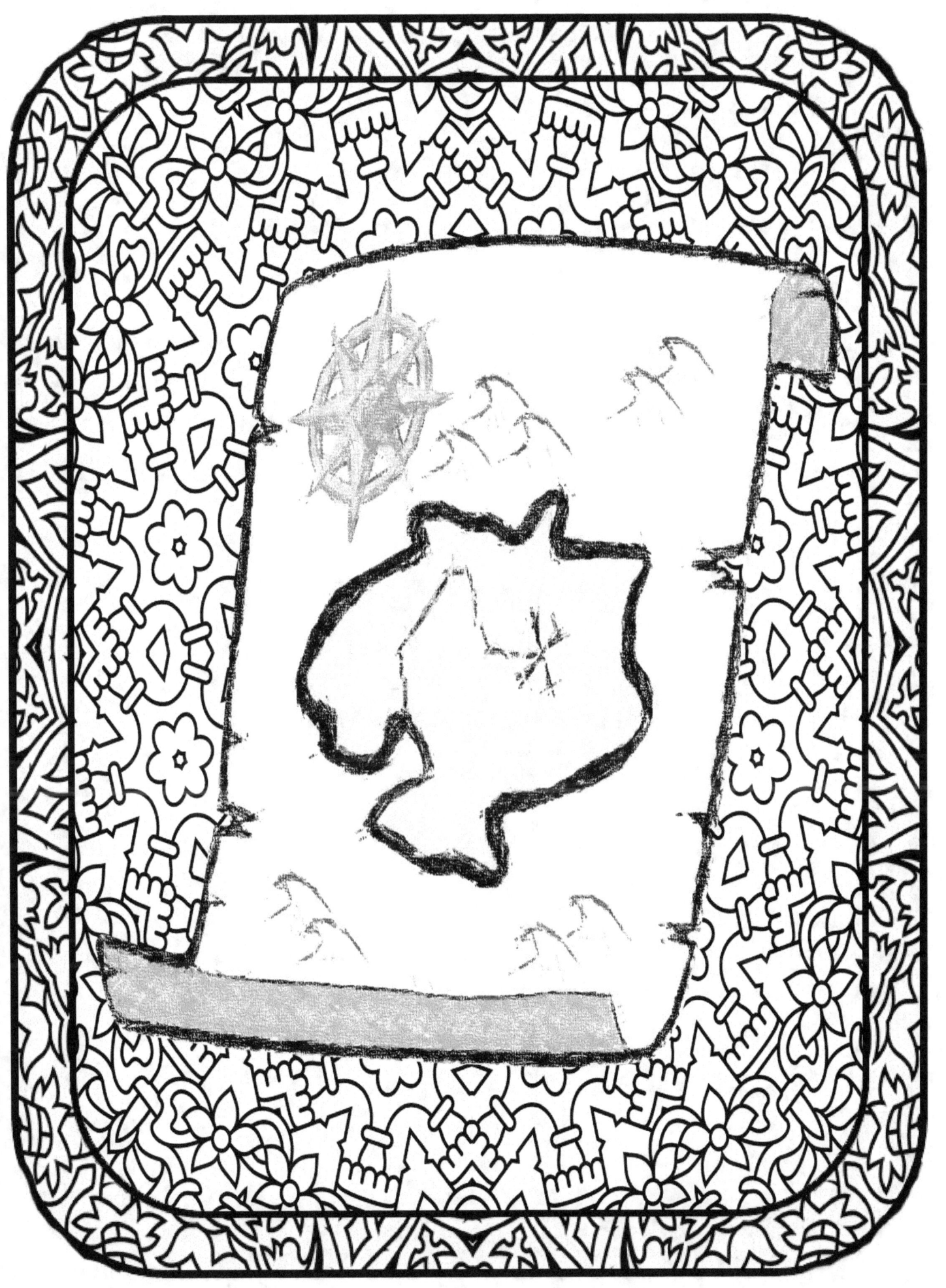

THINGS A PIRATE WOULD SAY

ALL HANDS HOAY = EVERYONE GET ON THE DECK
AVAST YE = PAY ATTENTION
BLACK SPOT = DEATH THREAT
DANCE THE HEMPEN JIG = TO HANG SOMEONE
DUNGBIE = REAR END
HEMPEN HALTER = THE NOOSE USED TO HANG PEOPLE
HORNSWAGGLE = TO CHEAT
SHIVER ME TIMBERS = AN EXPRESSION USED TO SHOW SHOCK OR DISBELIEF
ABAFT = BACK AREA OF THE BOAT
BINNACLE = WHERE THE COMPASS IS KEPT ON BOARD THE SHIP
CACKLE FRUIT = CHICKEN EGGS
COAMING = A SURFACE THAT PREVENTED WATER ON THE DECK FROM DRIPPING TO LOWER LEVELS OF THE SHIP

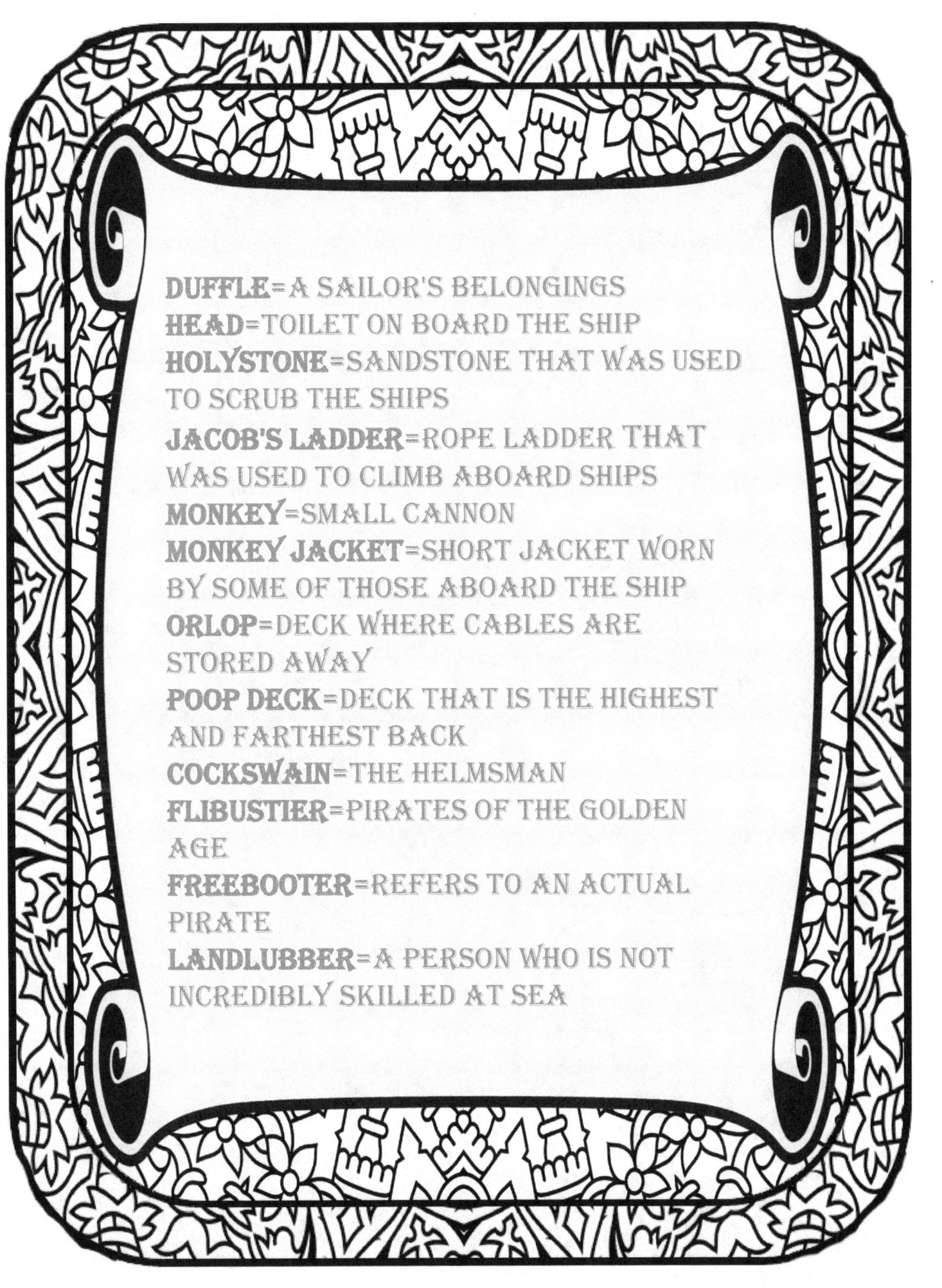

DUFFLE=A SAILOR'S BELONGINGS
HEAD=TOILET ON BOARD THE SHIP
HOLYSTONE=SANDSTONE THAT WAS USED TO SCRUB THE SHIPS
JACOB'S LADDER=ROPE LADDER THAT WAS USED TO CLIMB ABOARD SHIPS
MONKEY=SMALL CANNON
MONKEY JACKET=SHORT JACKET WORN BY SOME OF THOSE ABOARD THE SHIP
ORLOP=DECK WHERE CABLES ARE STORED AWAY
POOP DECK=DECK THAT IS THE HIGHEST AND FARTHEST BACK
COCKSWAIN=THE HELMSMAN
FLIBUSTIER=PIRATES OF THE GOLDEN AGE
FREEBOOTER=REFERS TO AN ACTUAL PIRATE
LANDLUBBER=A PERSON WHO IS NOT INCREDIBLY SKILLED AT SEA

POWDER MONKEY = A GUNNER'S ASSISTANT
BLACK JACK = LARGE DRINKING CUPS
DAVY JONES' LOCKER = REFERS TO DEATH
AHOY = HELLO
AHOY, MATEY = HELLO, FRIEND
BATTEN DOWN THE HATCHES = A SIGNAL TO PREPARE THE SHIP FOR AN UPCOMING STORM
BLIMEY! = SOMETHING SAID WHEN ONE IS IN A STATE OF SURPRISE
BLOW THE MAN DOWN = A COMMAND WHICH MEANS TO KILL SOMEBODY
BOOTY = TREASURE
BUCCANEER = NAME FOR A PIRATE
CROW'S NEST = THE PLACE ON THE SHIP WHERE THE LOOKOUT STAND IS BUILT
CUTLASS = TYPE OF SWORD USED BY THE PIRATES

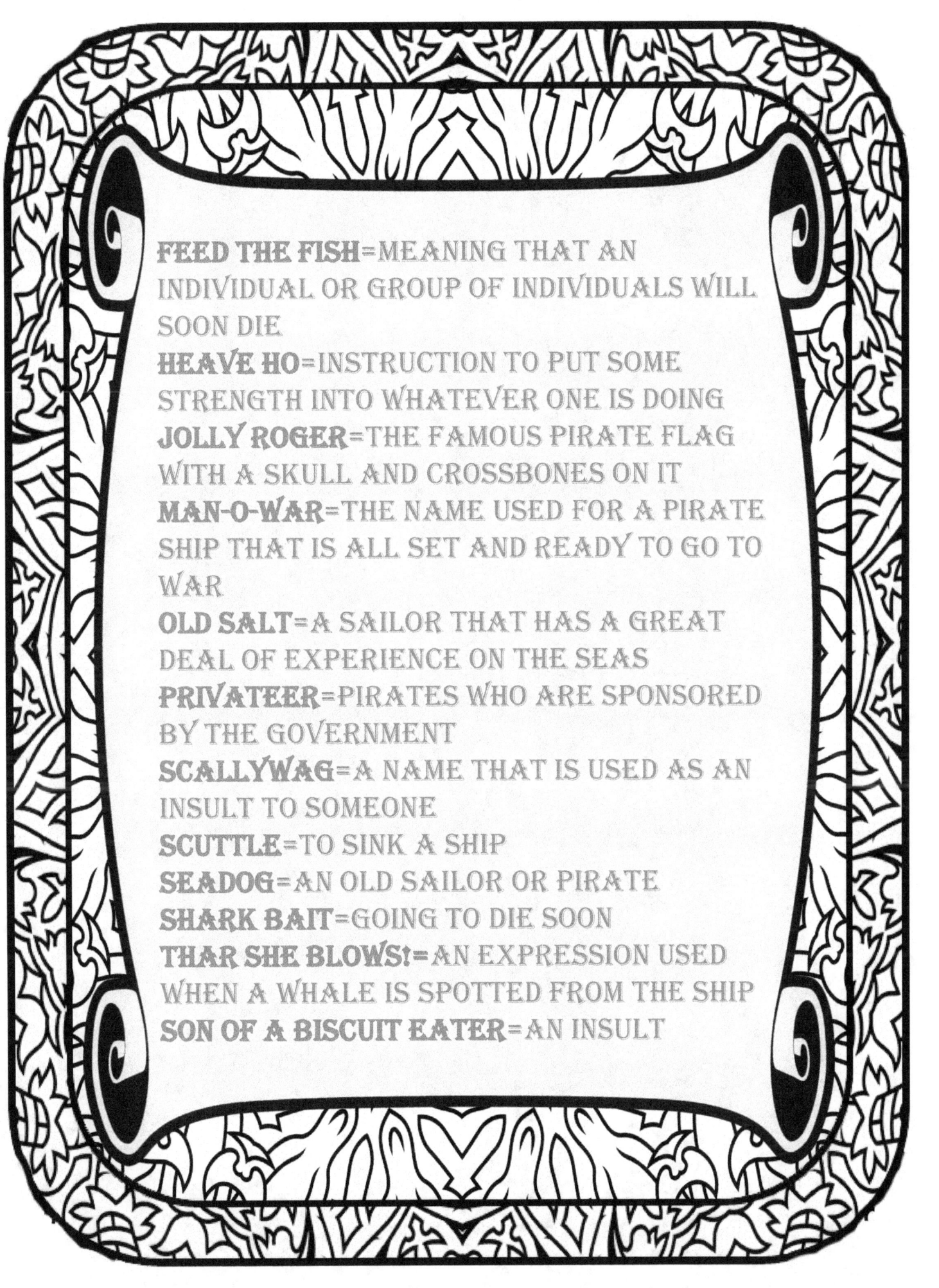

FEED THE FISH = MEANING THAT AN INDIVIDUAL OR GROUP OF INDIVIDUALS WILL SOON DIE

HEAVE HO = INSTRUCTION TO PUT SOME STRENGTH INTO WHATEVER ONE IS DOING

JOLLY ROGER = THE FAMOUS PIRATE FLAG WITH A SKULL AND CROSSBONES ON IT

MAN-O-WAR = THE NAME USED FOR A PIRATE SHIP THAT IS ALL SET AND READY TO GO TO WAR

OLD SALT = A SAILOR THAT HAS A GREAT DEAL OF EXPERIENCE ON THE SEAS

PRIVATEER = PIRATES WHO ARE SPONSORED BY THE GOVERNMENT

SCALLYWAG = A NAME THAT IS USED AS AN INSULT TO SOMEONE

SCUTTLE = TO SINK A SHIP

SEADOG = AN OLD SAILOR OR PIRATE

SHARK BAIT = GOING TO DIE SOON

THAR SHE BLOWS! = AN EXPRESSION USED WHEN A WHALE IS SPOTTED FROM THE SHIP

SON OF A BISCUIT EATER = AN INSULT

THREE SHEETS TO THE WIND = SOMEONE WHO IS QUITE DRUNK

WALK THE PLANK = A PUNISHMENT WHICH ENTAILS SOMEONE WHO WALKS OVER THE SIDE OF THE SHIP OFF OF THE PLANK. THEIR HANDS ARE OFTEN TIED SO THAT THEY CANNOT SWIM AND THEY DROWNED.

YO HO HO = THERE IS OFTEN USED TO EXPRESS SOME SORT OF CHEER BUT ALSO CAN BE USED TO CALL ATTENTION TO THE SPEAKER.

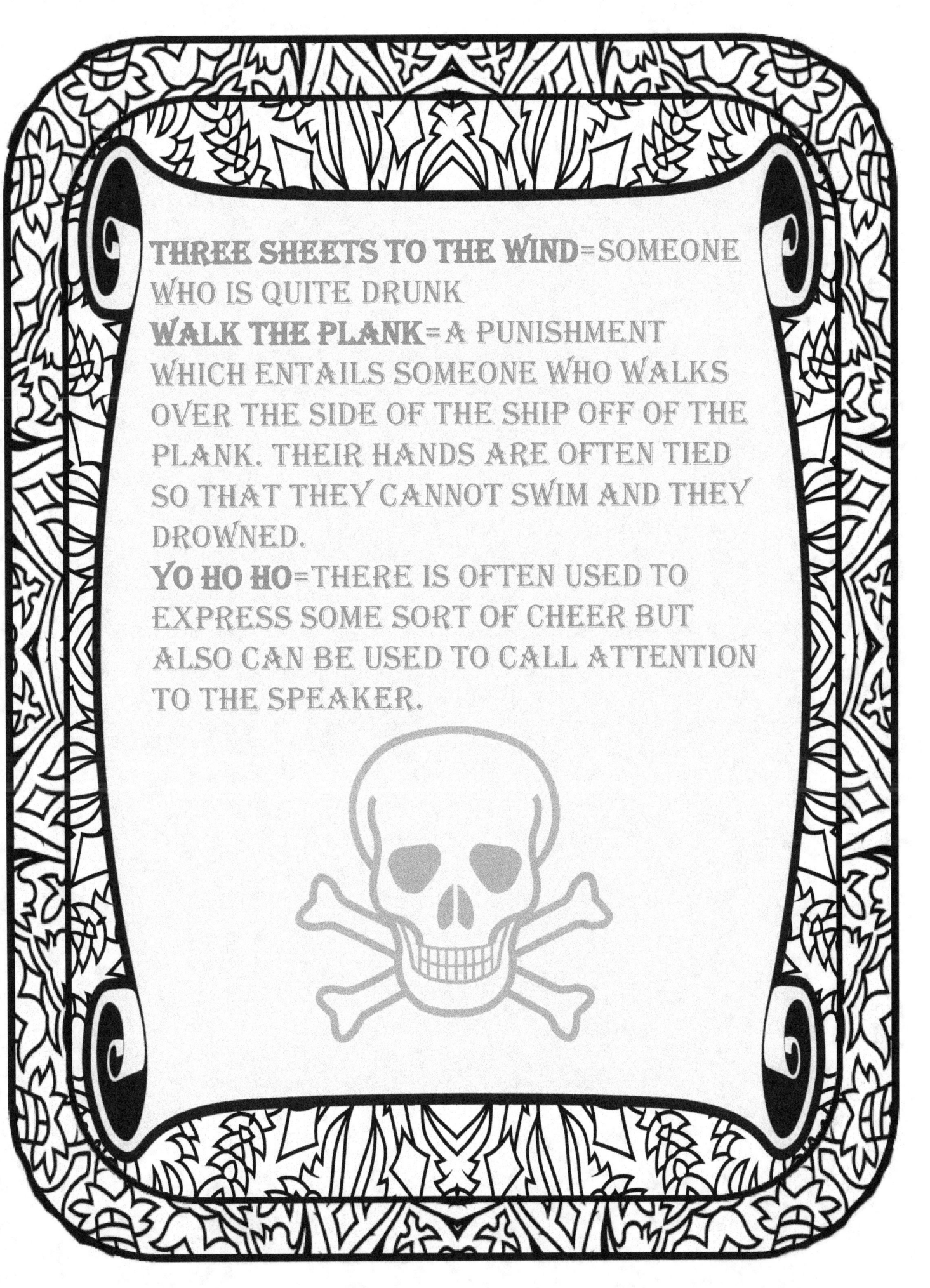

20 MAZES

MAZE 1

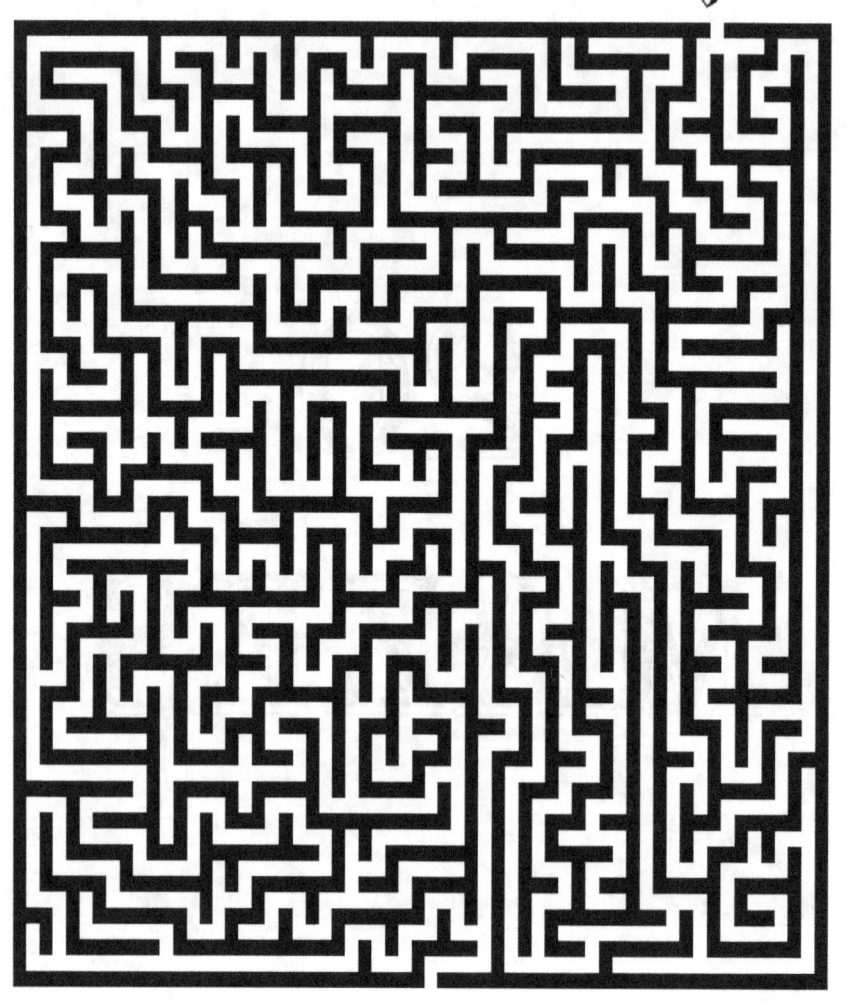
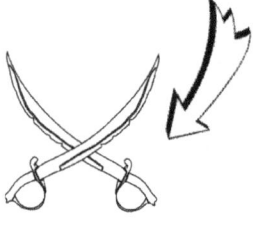

MAZE 2

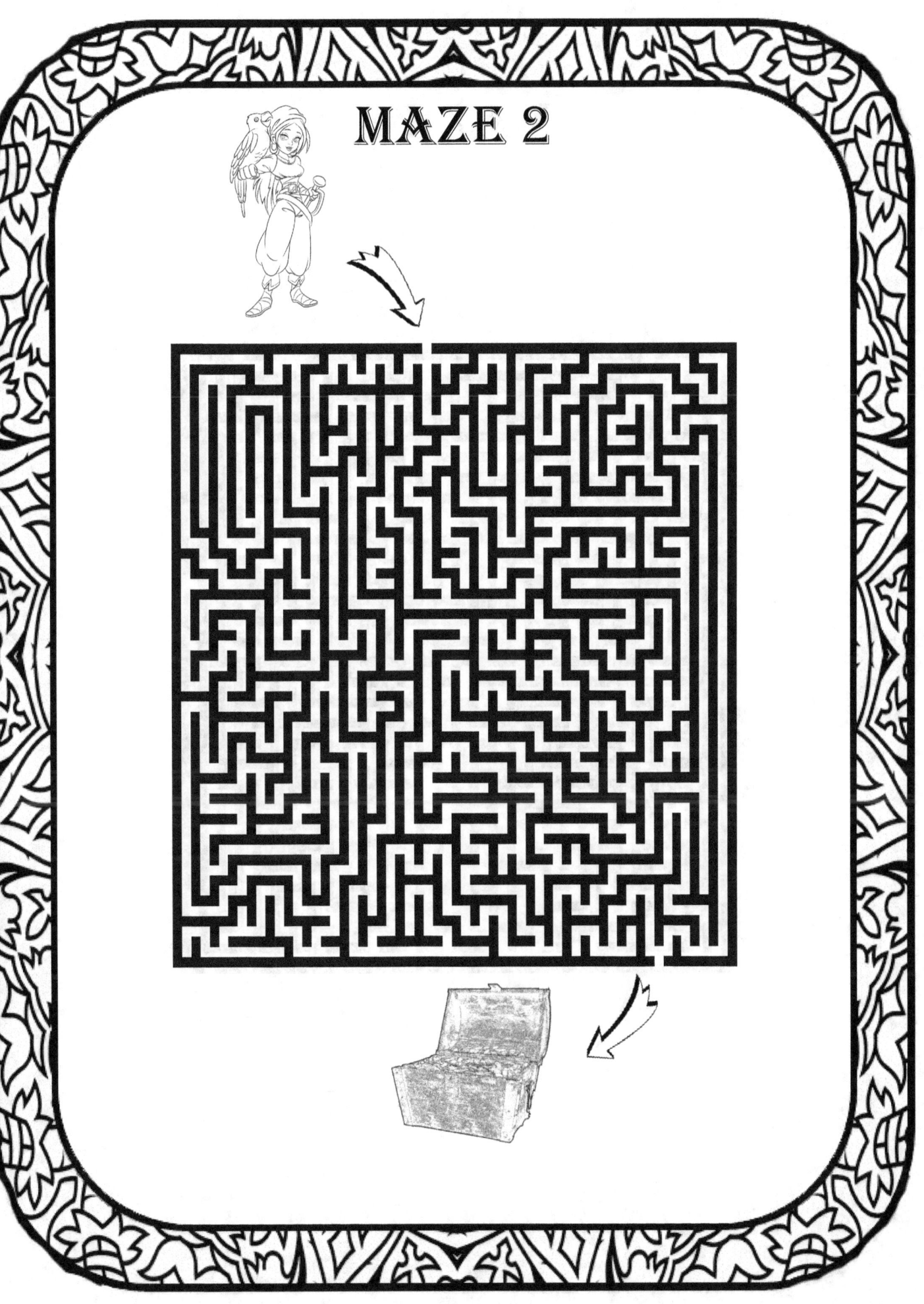

MAZE 3

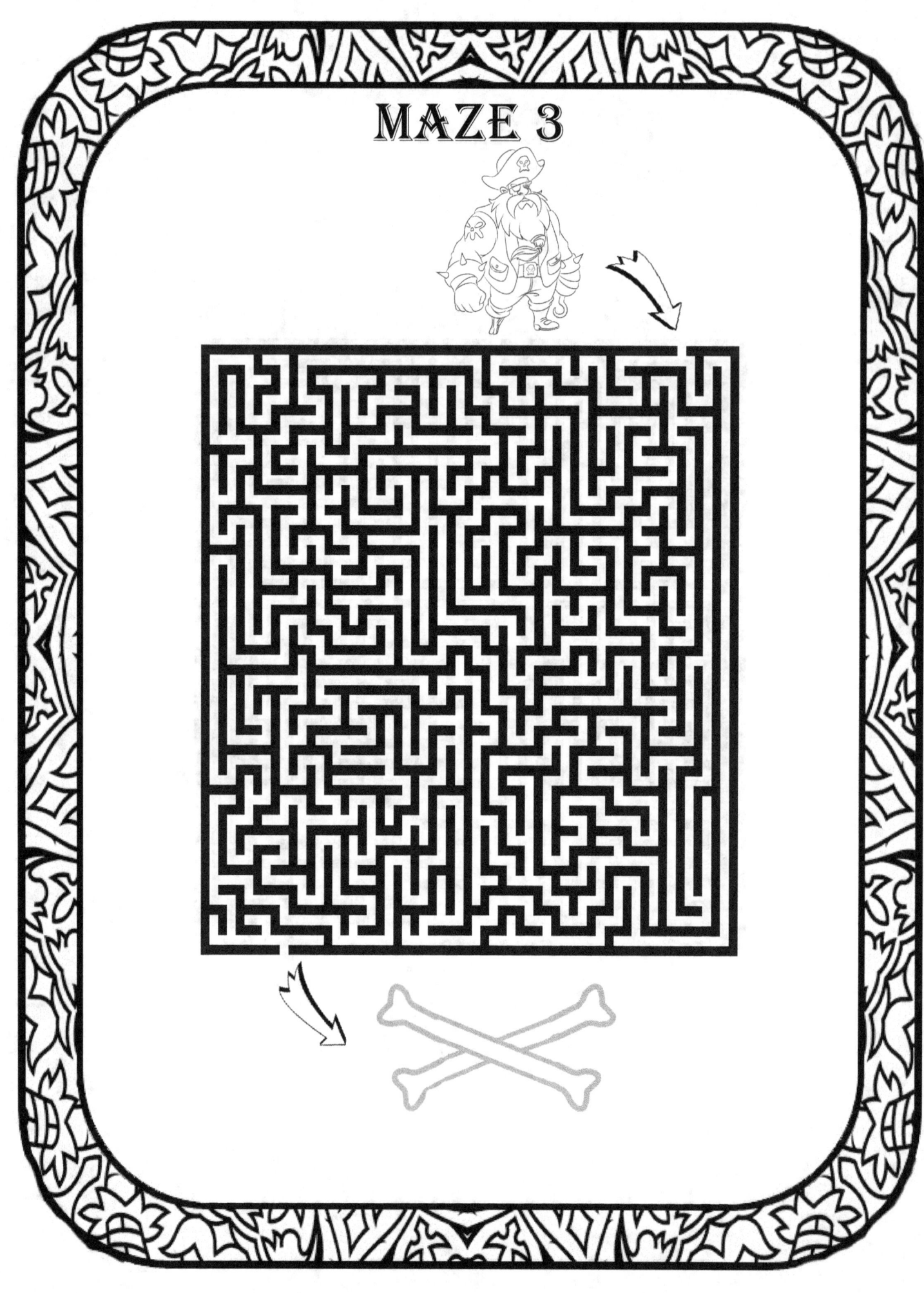

MAZE 4

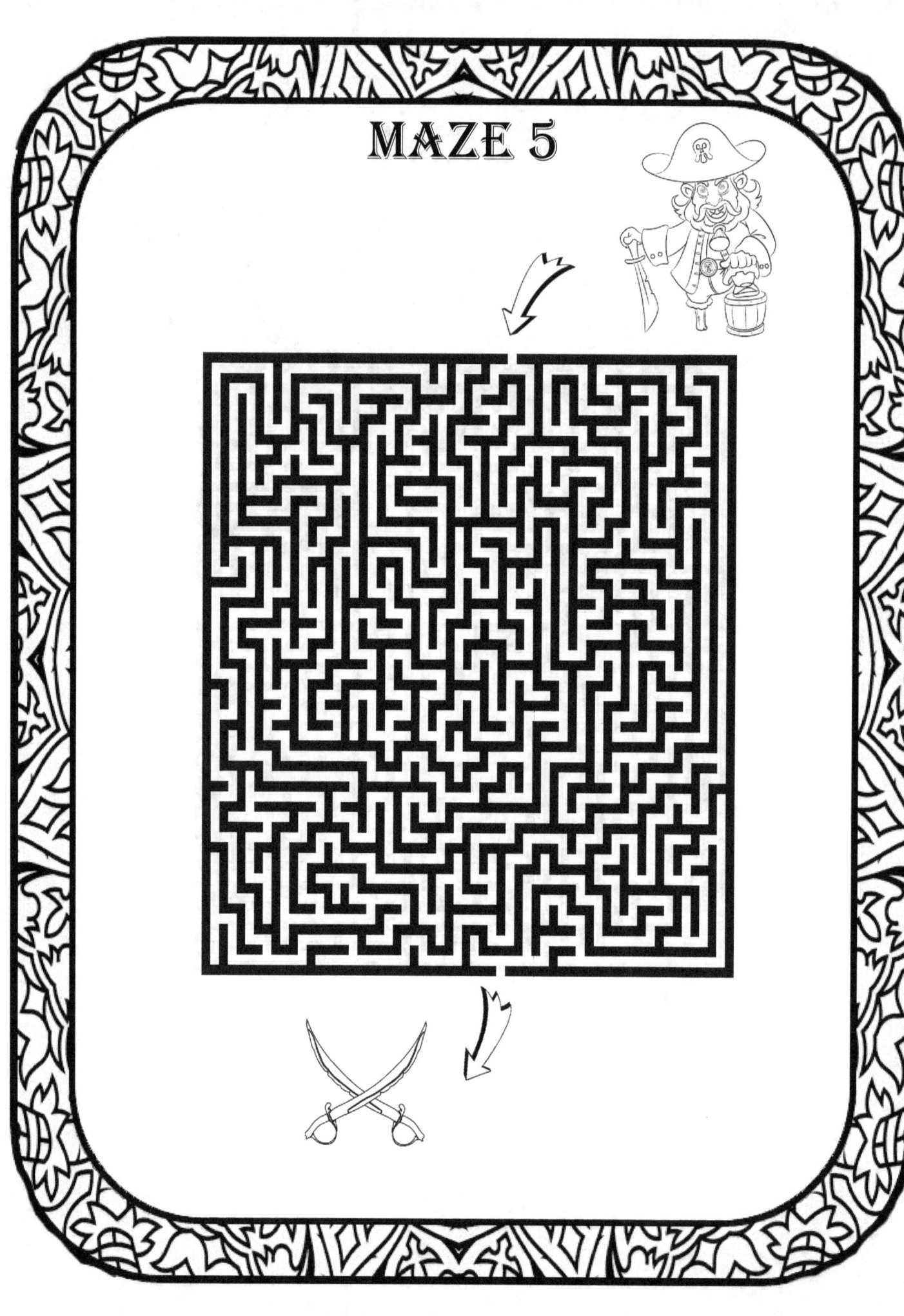

MAZE 6

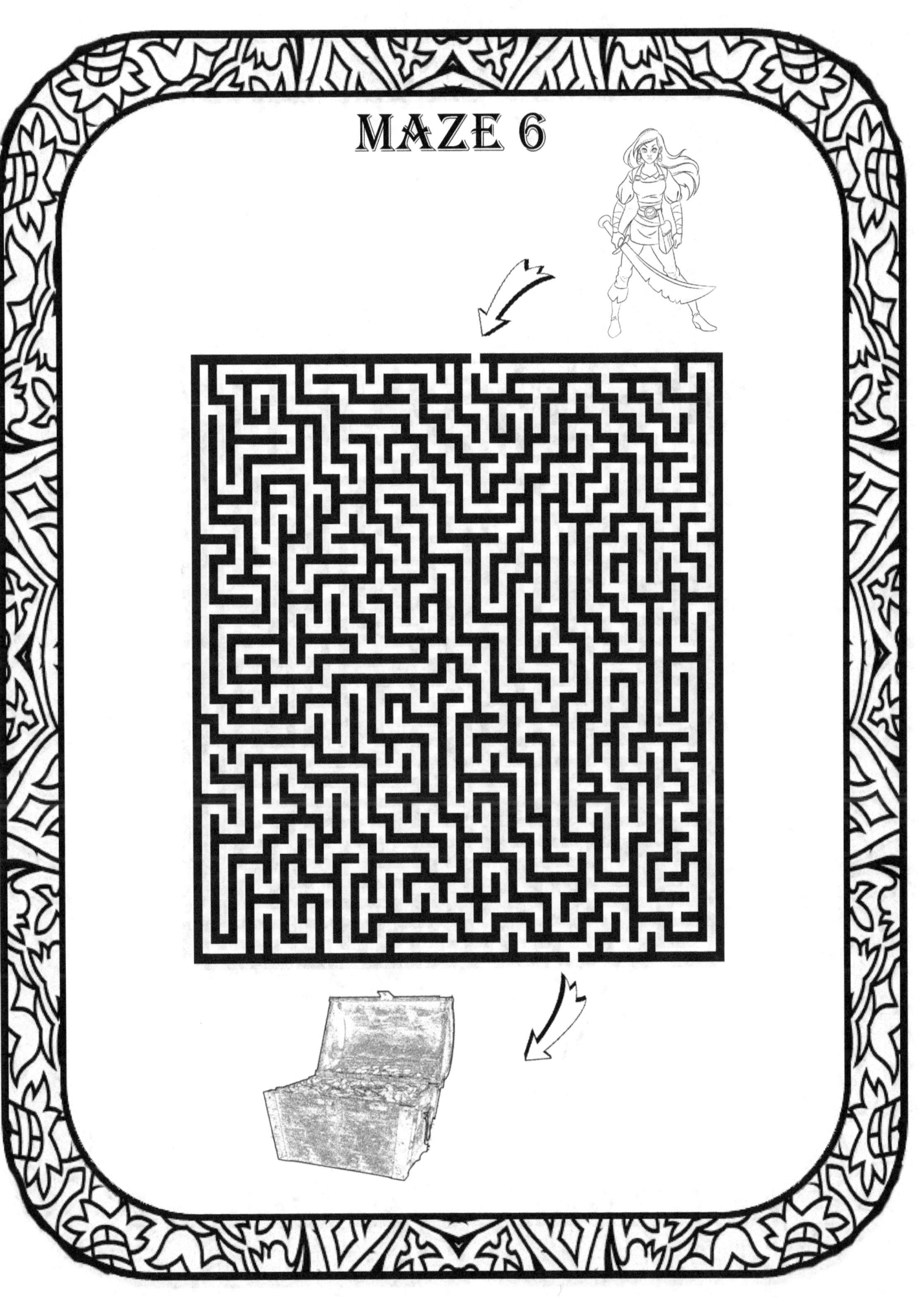

MAZE 7

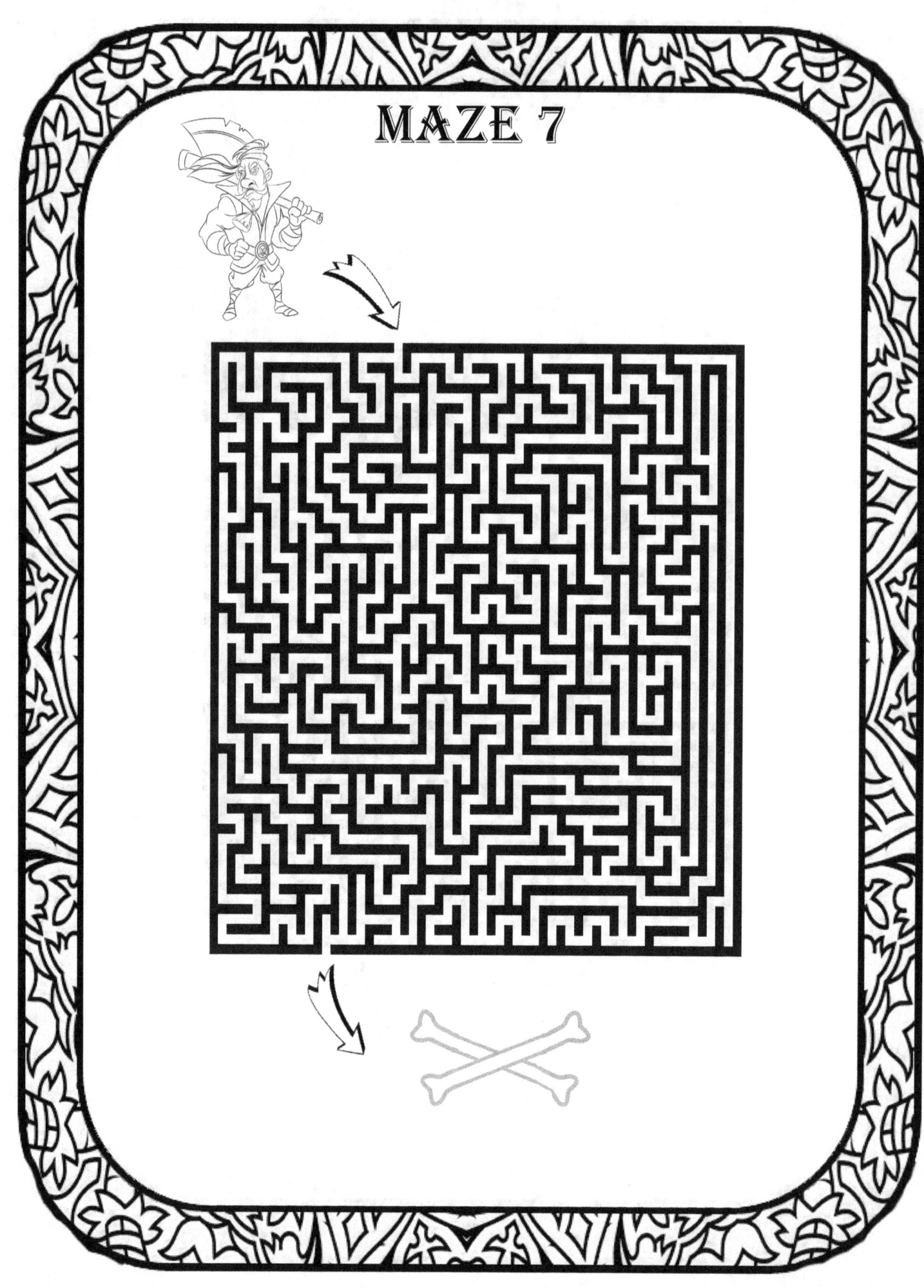

MAZE 8

MAZE 9

MAZE 10

MAZE 11

MAZE 12

MAZE 13

MAZE 14

MAZE 15

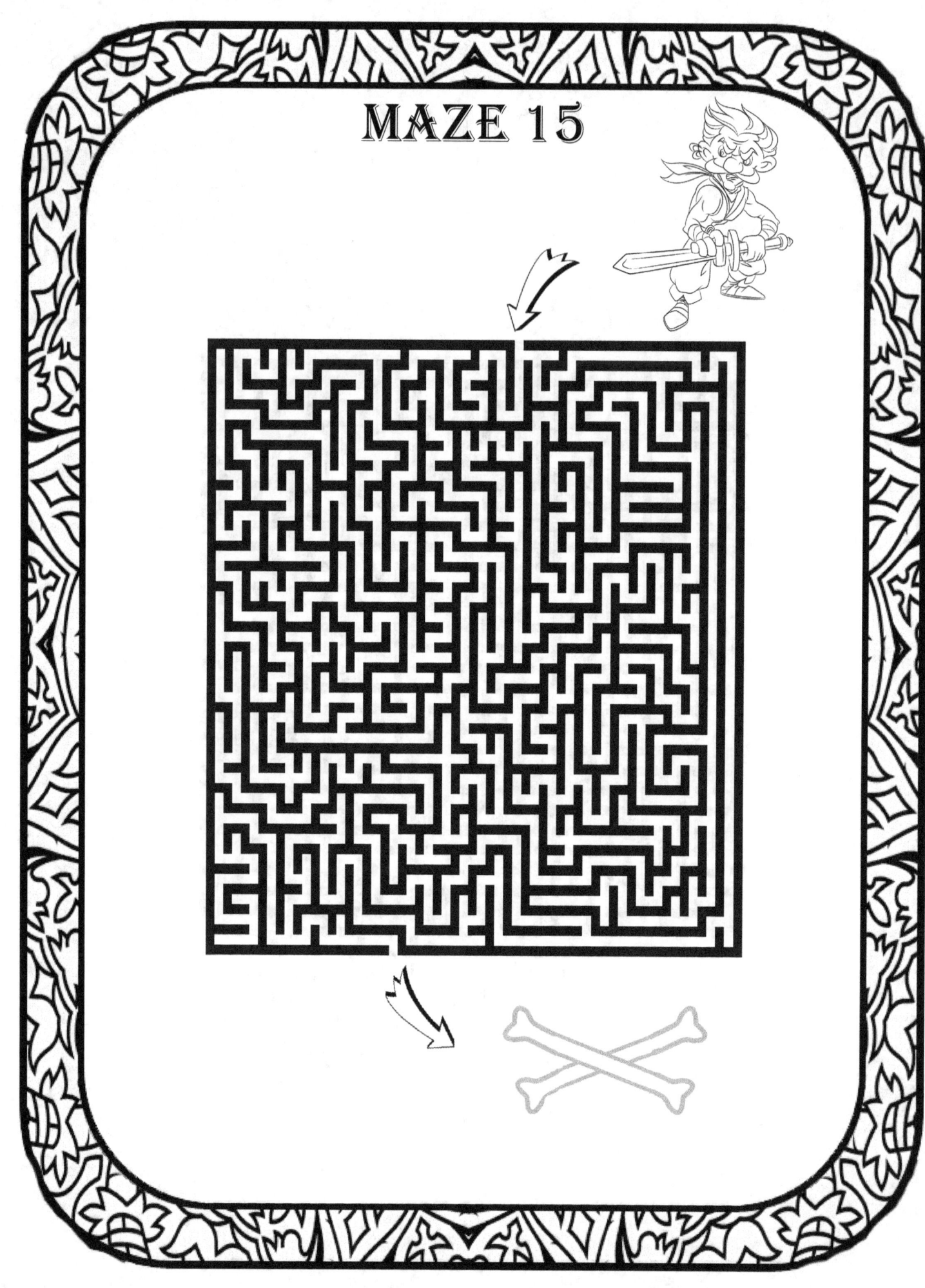

MAZE 16

MAZE 17

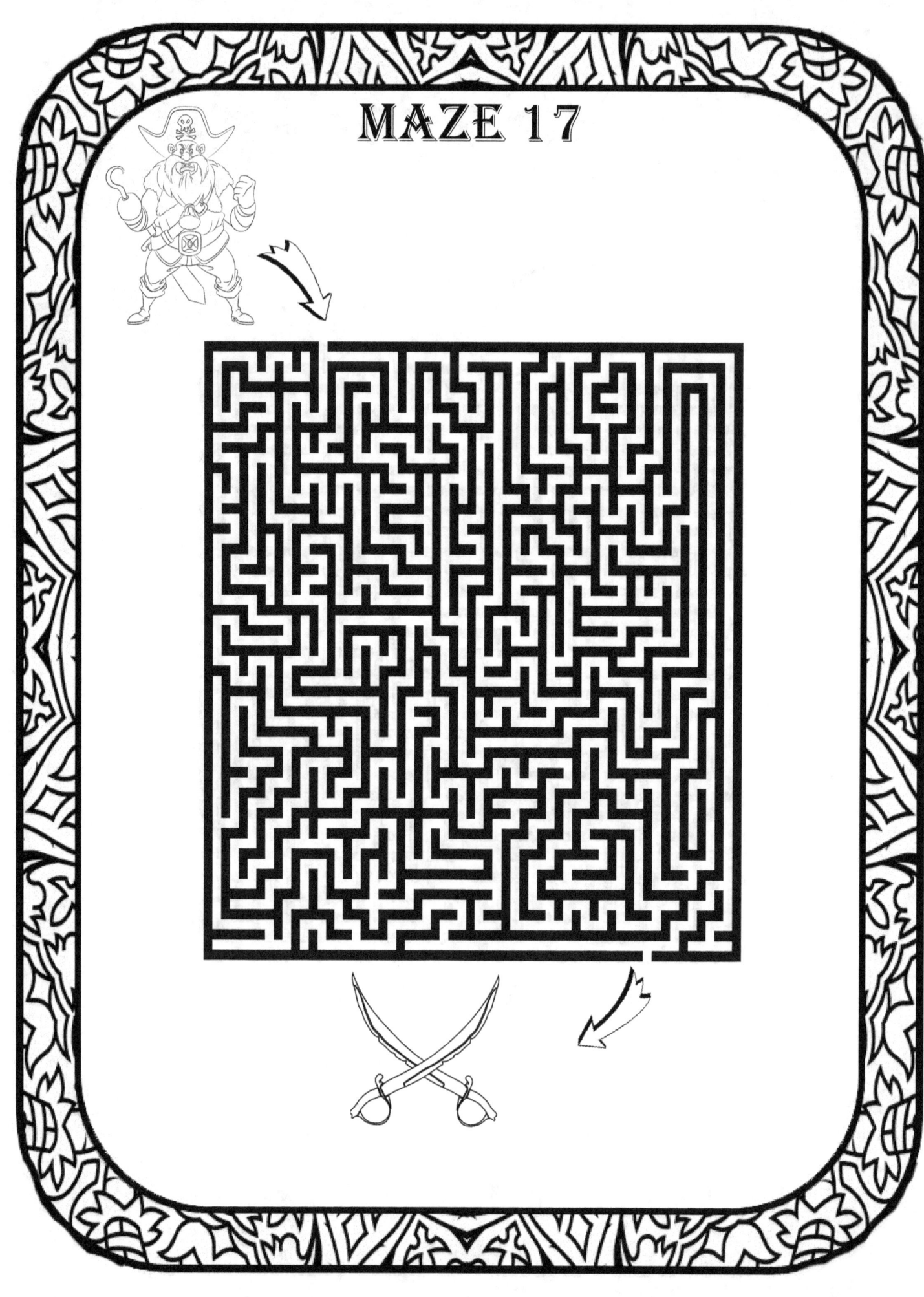

MAZE 18

MAZE 19

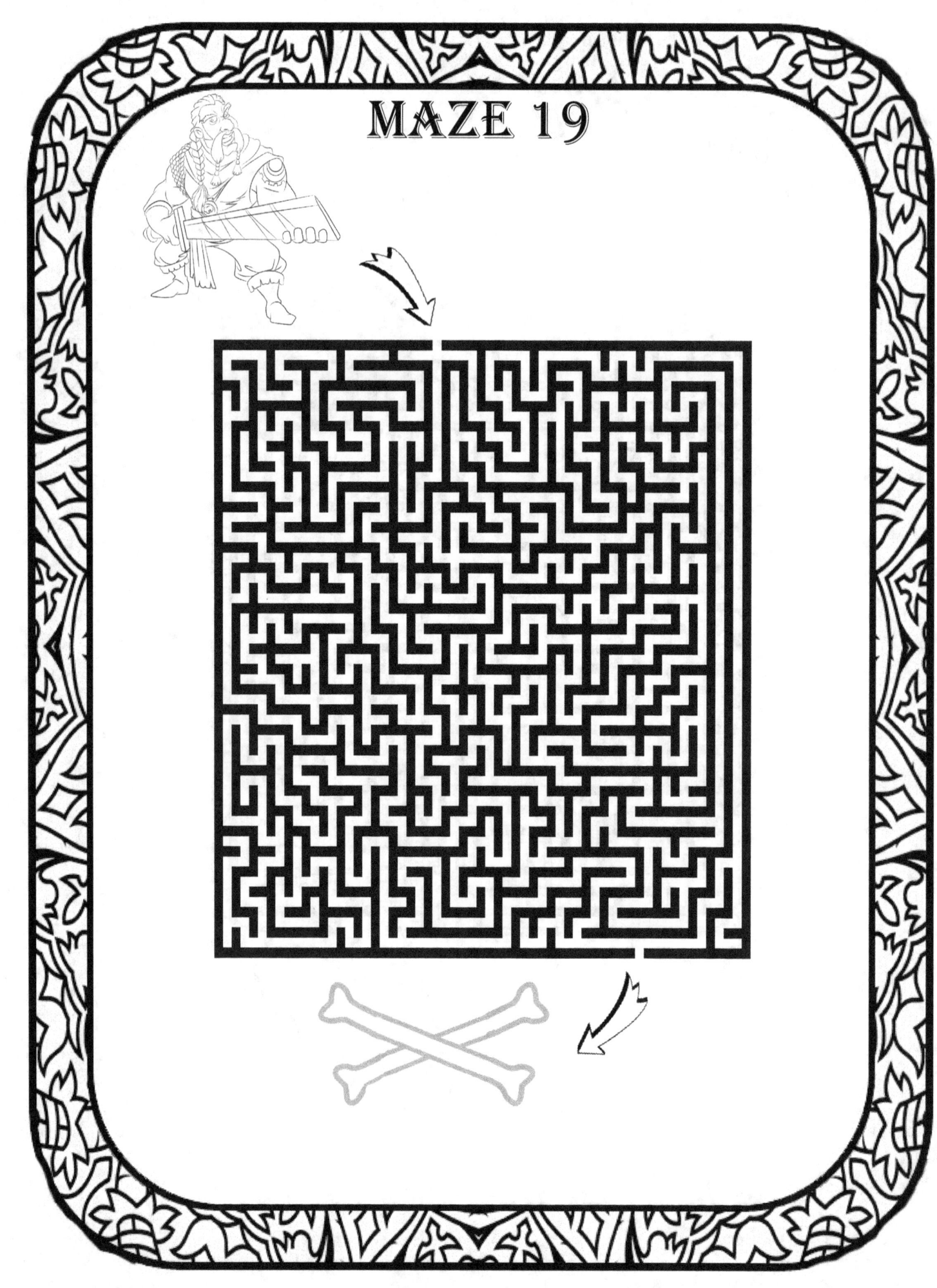

MAZE 20

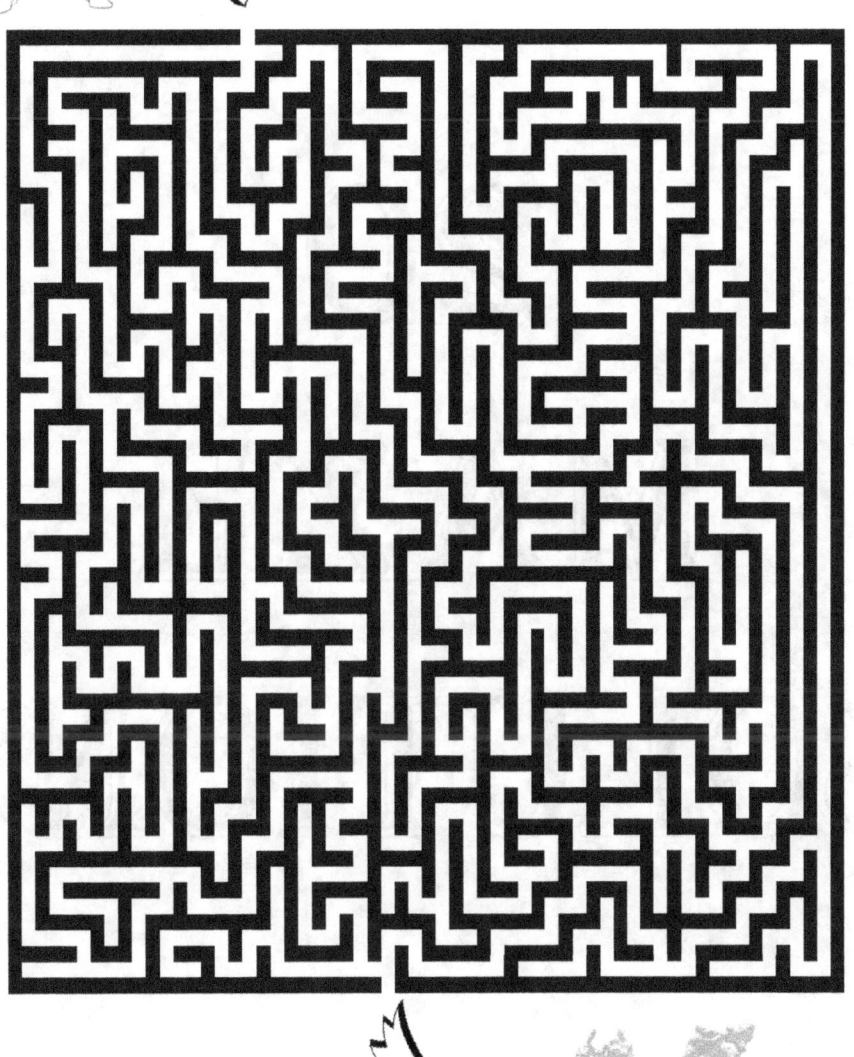

20 MAZE SOLUTIONS

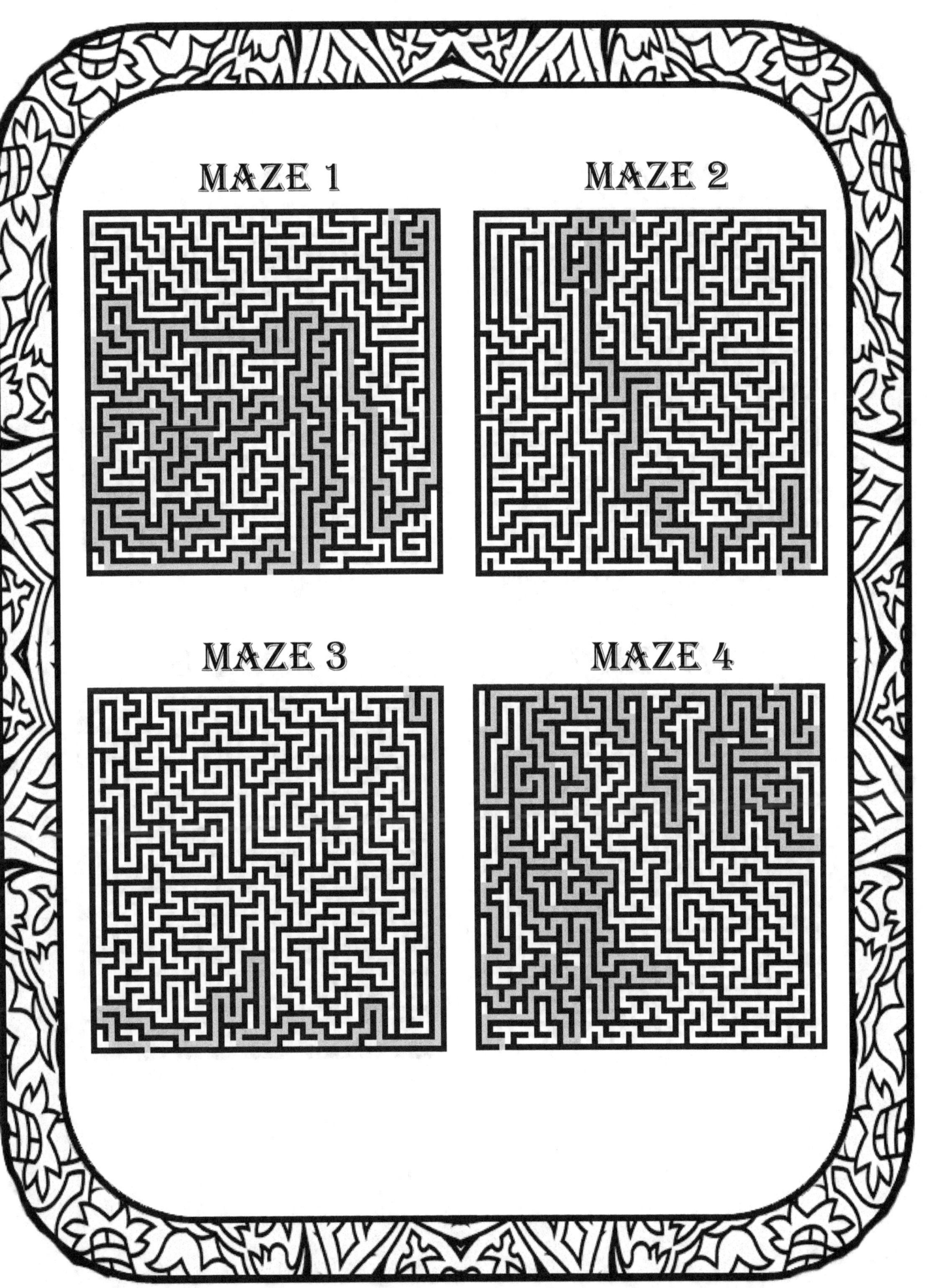

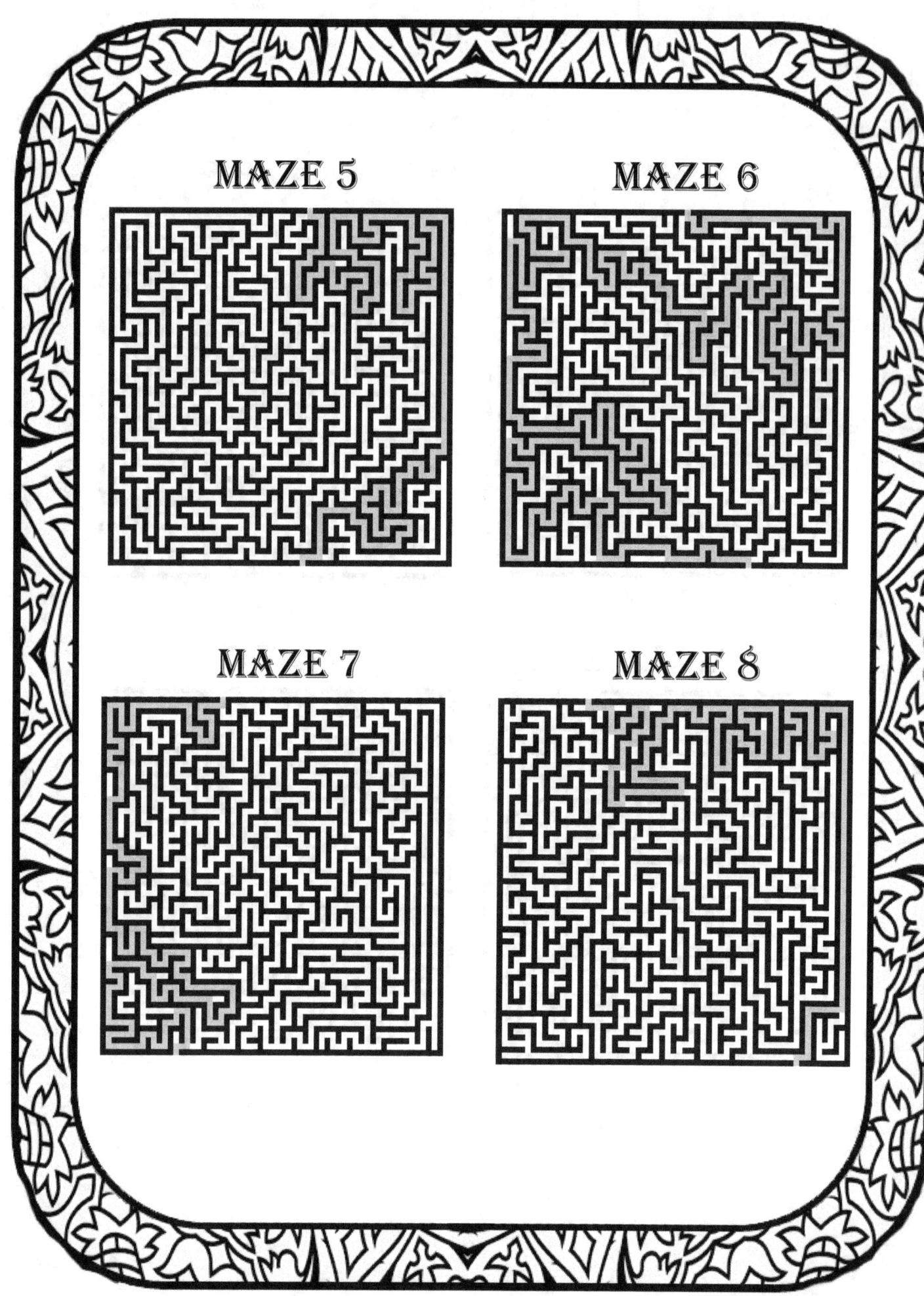

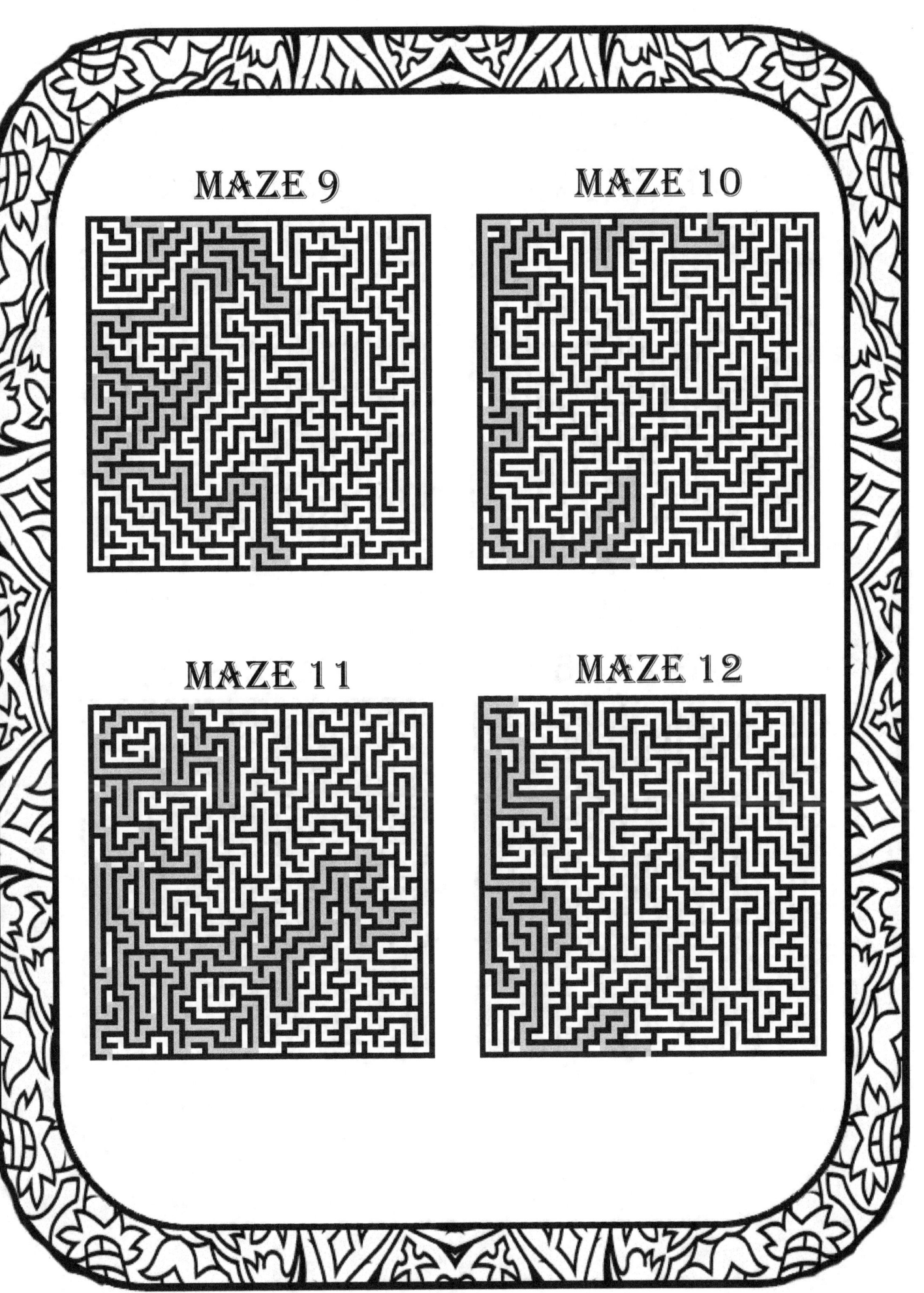

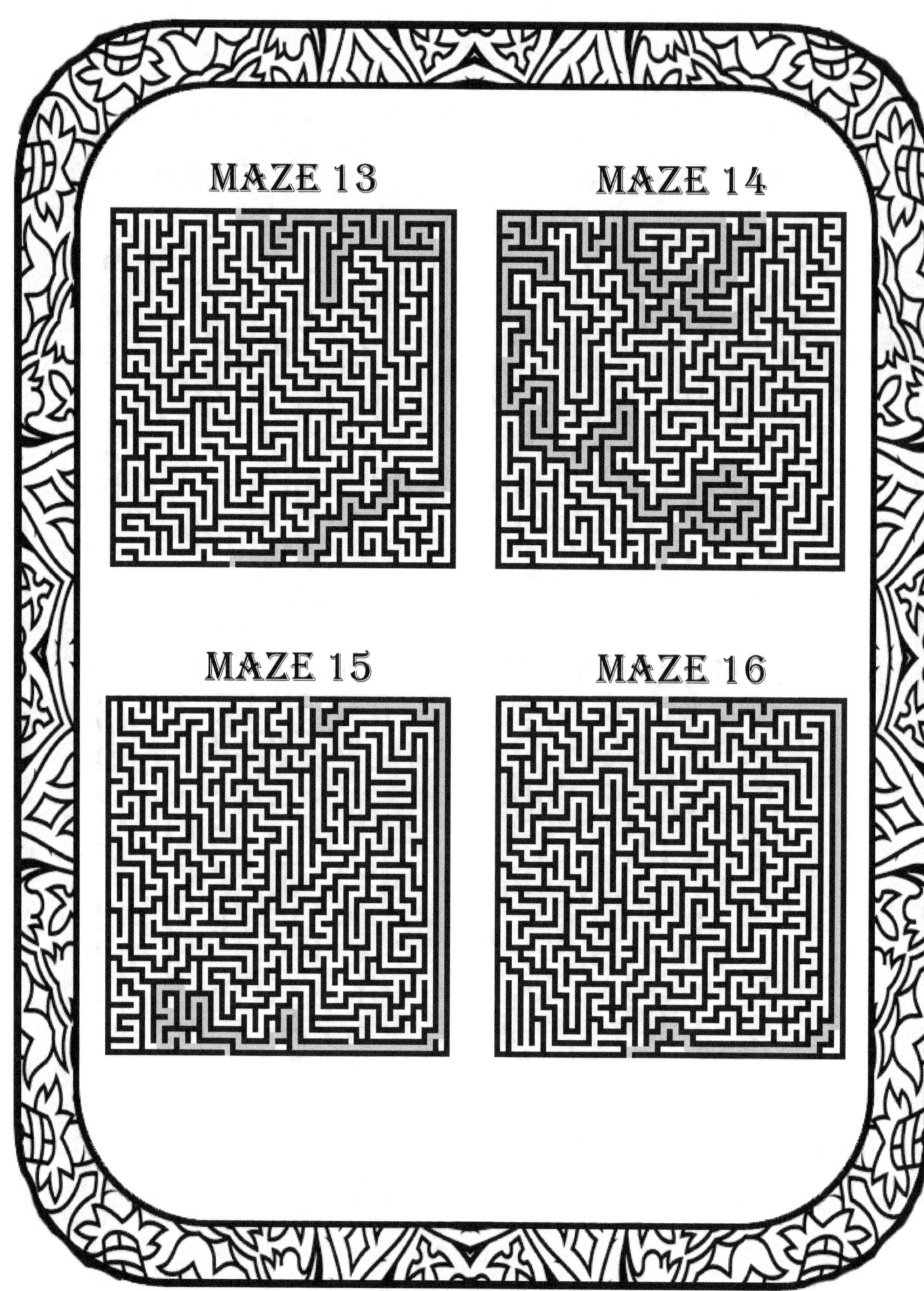

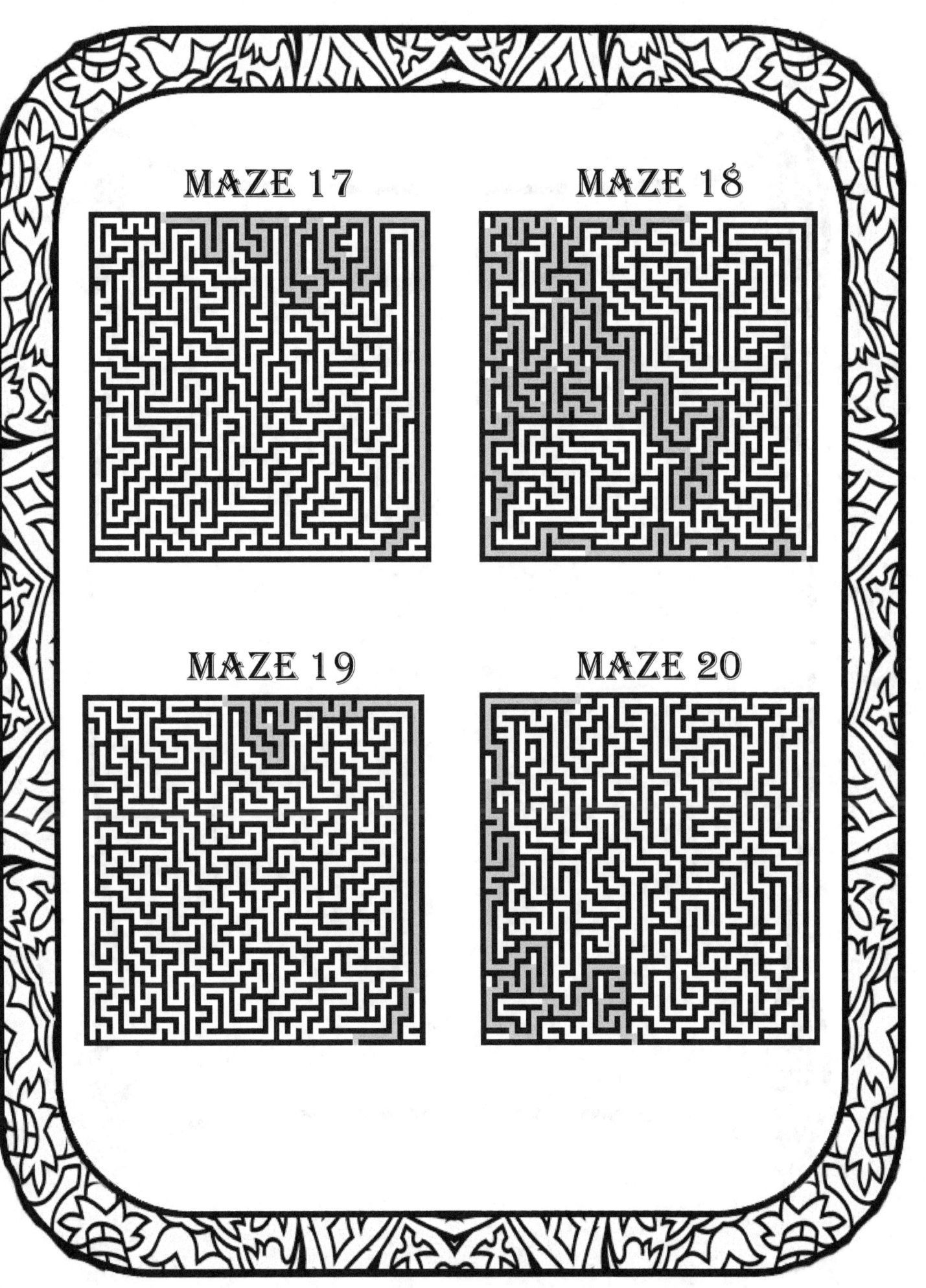

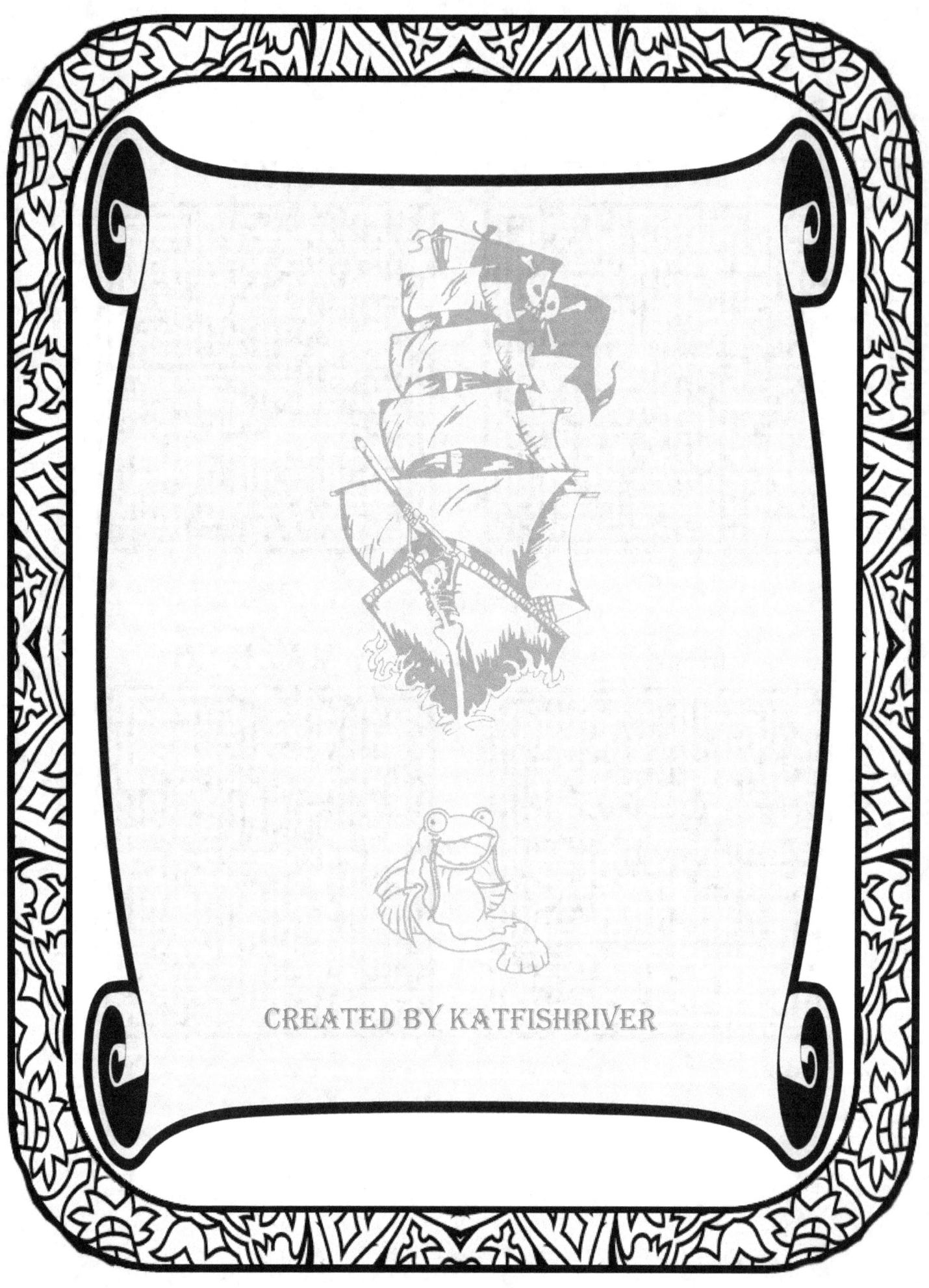